Embroiderer's Basic Tool Kit

- Thread
- Needles
- Fabric
- Embroidery scissors
- Dressmaker shears
- Thimbles
- Pincushions
- Embroidery
- Embroidery
- Needle threader
- Masking tape
- Dressmaker's carbon paper
- Frame

Name-Dropping: Stitches an Embroiderer Should Know

- Running
- Double running
- Satin
- Stem
- Straight
- Basic cross
- Chain
- Blanket
- French knot

Techniques to Create Special Embroidery Effects

- Couching
- Laidwork
- Beadwork
- Smocking
- Crewelwork
- Stumpwork
- Whitework
- Blackwork

alpha books

tear here

Needlepointer's Basic Tool Kit

- Yarns
- Needles
- Canvas
- Frame
- Embroidery scissors
- Dressmaker's carbon paper
- Dressmaker shears
- Felt-tip marker
- Masking tape
- Acrylic paints
- Paintbrush

Name-Dropping: Stitches a Needlepointer Should Know

- Tent
- Slanted Gobelin
- Scottish
- Checker
- Cross
- Upright Gobelin
- Large Algerian Eye
- Velvet

Techniques to Create Special Needlepoint Effects

- Bargello
- Blended tones
- Marbled backgrounds
- Unworked backgrounds
- Shading
- Raised effects

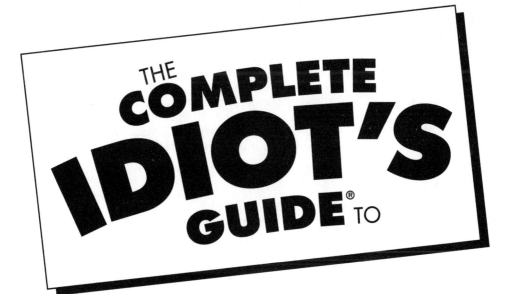

Needlework

by Mary Ann Young

**alpha
books**

Macmillan USA, Inc.
201 West 103rd Street
Indianapolis, IN 46290

A Pearson Education Company

Publisher
Marie Butler-Knight

Product Manager
Phil Kitchel

Managing Editor
Cari Luna

Acquisitions Editor
Amy Zavatto

Development Editor
Amy Gordon

Senior Production Editor
Christy Wagner

Copy Editor
Diana Francoeur

Illustrator
Jody Schaeffer

Cover Designers
Mike Freeland
Kevin Spear

Book Designers
Scott Cook and Amy Adams of DesignLab

Indexer
Lisa Wilson

Layout/Proofreading
John Etchison
Steve Geiselman

Contents at a Glance

Contents

Appendixes

Foreword

Embroidery is an age-old and beloved art that began, we think, in prehistoric times, when man decided to decorate his clothing and other belongings. Bits and scraps of embroidery have been found in ancient Egyptian and Chinese tombs. Embroidery is mentioned in the Old Testament, and it has been prominent in religious decoration through the ages. We see it proudly worn in portraits and displayed on samplers. Needlepoint, a form of embroidery, has also been popular since early times.

I began stitching as a child. My mother felt that if I was sick and had to stay home from school that I should be in bed. Since I was an active child, in order to keep me there she would give me squares of cloth that were printed with cross stitch or outline designs and several skeins of thread. Her scheme worked. I lay there and stitched or read and then stitched some more until she felt it was time for me to go back to school. Later she taught me to needlepoint so I could help her with some chair seats she was making. Stitching has always been part of my life; I can't imagine not doing it. But it has changed over the years.

Today's embroidery and needlepoint are tremendously exciting. There are wonderful new threads, fabrics, and canvasses to be used, along with the traditional linens, silks, wools, and cottons. There are myriad colors to choose from, both to stitch with and to stitch on. There are kits, painted canvases, graphs, design books—a wealth of items from which to choose. There is an unlimited number of ways to use your finished embroidered or needlepointed piece, from chair seats, pillows, and pictures, to boxes, jewelry, clothing, and holiday ornaments—almost anything can be embellished with your embroidery and will add warmth and individuality.

But if you've never done any embroidery before, where to begin? *The Complete Idiot's Guide to Needlework* by Mary Ann Young contains much good, basic information that will help you to get started in the exciting world of embroidery and needlepoint. Her directions are easy to understand, and she takes you from the beginning to the finishing of a piece of embroidery or needlepoint. Reading and working with this book will surely draw you into the wonderful world of embroidery and needlepoint.

It's a world of color and texture, where fabric and threads become the tools to create art, and you will be the artist who is creating an embroidery that will be treasured and enjoyed for generations. Pick up your needle and begin to stitch—join all those needleworkers who have found fulfillment through this form of self-expression. It is a true joy.

If you find that you really like to stitch and would like to delve further into this art, you will find a wonderful resource in The Embroiderers' Guild of America, Inc. (familiarly and affectionately known as EGA). EGA is a nonprofit, educational, 20,000-member organization with about 350 chapters in the United States. It has correspondence courses, classes, seminars, a quarterly magazine, and is open to anyone who is interested in embroidery.

Embroidery can be a passion. It is with me. You can stitch with colored yarns or threads or work strictly in white. You can create a great deal of texture or keep your stitching relatively smooth. You can work with only one stitch or use a lot of different stitches. You can work on a large scale, or you can work tiny stitches on a tiny piece of fabric. I love to look at embroidery, I love to touch it, I love to read about it—but above all I love to do it.

Mary Lou Storrs
President, The Embroiderers' Guild of America, Inc.

For further information on The Embroiderers' Guild of America, Inc., contact The Embroiderers' Guild of America, Inc., 335 West Broadway, Suite 100, Louisville, KY 40202; www.egausa.com.

Introduction

First and foremost, a new hobby is meant to be fun! The interest and passion come first, and the learning and skill follow. Consider all of the needlework that you can accomplish in your life if you persevere in your new hobby. Take time to observe, learn, read about, practice, and—most of all—enjoy your embroidery and needlepoint. Discover and define your personal style through your use of color and texture with patterns and your own designs.

Although embroidery is a bit more difficult than needlepoint, I will teach you this form of needlework first, since needlepoint is a form of embroidery. Once you've learned the ins and outs of embroidery, we'll move on to needlepoint.

Throughout this book, you will gather ideas about the many possibilities for needlework, including where to find inspiration for your own designs and what you can make with needlework. You will learn many of the stitches used in embroidery and needlepoint, the tools necessary for each craft, projects that you can start with, and finishing techniques to give your piece a professional look.

Here are what I consider my most important principles of needlework. Keeping these in mind will make your needlework projects more exciting, rewarding, and creative! Read them over and try to remember them while you are in the beginner stage:

> ➤ **Forget about perfection.** People are not perfect, and needlework does not have to be, either! Don't obsess about being one stitch off or accidentally using the wrong color. Some of the most cherished works have stitching "flaws" that impart personal charm.

> ➤ **Be passionate about your hobby.** Let your style loose! Indulge in tastes of needlework that tempt you, and experiment with techniques that delight you. Stitch beauty with your needle. And showcase your lovely and beloved work in your home or wear it by adding it to your wardrobe!

> ➤ **Be practical and realistic.** Don't try to stitch a carpet that would fit in the Taj Mahal on your first try at needlework! Assess your time, finances, and the size of your home! Start small to get used to your materials and to encourage yourself to complete your work. Choose something that you love and will use for your project!

> ➤ **Let your style break the rules.** You will observe a lot of conventional needlework that is okay but somewhat uninteresting. Don't cling to design ideas that you think you have to follow: Give your imagination and your intuition free rein! Remember, you make up the rules for your needlework style!

How to Use This Book

Let's be honest: Even though successful needlework can be full of creativity, self-expression, artistry, and fun, it doesn't always feel that way. Learning and doing needlework in the midst of busy lives can be demanding, and time consuming. Certain projects require more time and money than you have! You need to make decisions about what kind of needlework projects fit into your lifestyle, skill level, and budget! It is a constant process of discovering, learning, and testing.

This book is designed to help make learning embroidery and needlepoint a joy. It will get you started in the right direction so that you can't wait to gather your supplies and get stitching.

Here's how the book is organized:

Part 1, "Welcome to Needlecrafts," is for all needleworkers. Start here to get a good idea of how needlework began, its impact on the past, and how we use it today. You'll also find the basics on design to help you be a better needleworker with an eye for color, scale, texture, and balance.

Part 2, "Embroidery Basics," allows you to get a head start on embroidery by learning about the basic tools, basic techniques, and basic stitches.

Part 3, "Advanced Embroidery," takes you to the next level with special stitches that have special effects. You'll learn what is involved in designing your own patterns and what it takes to finish and complete a project. To test your skill, there are specific instructions from start to finish for a simple sampler to embroider!

Part 4, "Needlepoint Basics," allows you to get started in the wonderful world of needlepoint. From the tools to the tips and tricks of the trade to many stitches and particular designs, this part is chock full of information!

Part 5, "Advanced Needlepoint," shows you some techniques, additional designs, and finishing processes to get you on your way to becoming a master of the subject. You will be able to start and complete a simple dollhouse rug from start to finish. This will allow you to get used to the materials and stitching.

Part 6, "Getting Crafty," points out many of the ways that needlework can work for you! You will see how to take your craft to a new level and learn how to share your knowledge with others.

A Little Help Along the Way

I highlight some of the best, simplest, and most important ideas throughout the book in the special featured notes. Some of these are necessary for every needleworker to know, some are helpful tips, and others will warn you against pitfalls.

Needlework 101

These boxes contain needlework definitions that will help you speak needlework lingo.

A Stitch in Time

Needlework tips to keep you on your toes can be found in these boxes.

Decorator's Do's and Don'ts

These are warnings from a decorating pro that will keep you from design and practical disasters!

Clever Crafter

Clever Crafter boxes hold extra information of interest in the needlework world.

Acknowledgments

I would like to thank all of the people who made this book possible: Suzi Craig, whose tireless efforts, talent for words, and team spirit were much appreciated; Jill Reed Siroty at DMC Corporation; Linda and Kristen at JCA, Inc.; and Jo Parker at Laura Ashley.

Most of all, thanks to my acquisitions editor Amy Zavatto for giving me another chance at authorship!

Special Thanks to the Technical Reviewer

The Complete Idiot's Guide to Needlework was reviewed by an expert who double-checked the accuracy of what you'll learn here, to help us ensure that this book gives you everything you need to know about needlework. Special thanks are extended to Stephanie Tybaert.

Trademarks

All terms mentioned in this book that are known to be or are suspected of being trademarks or service marks have been appropriately capitalized. Alpha Books and Macmillan USA, Inc., cannot attest to the accuracy of this information. Use of a term in this book should not be regarded as affecting the validity of any trademark or service mark.

Part 1

Welcome to Needlecrafts

Remember your first day of school? If you were like me, you couldn't wait to be a "big kid." What you didn't know at the time was that before you could graduate to big kid status, you had to learn the basics. No sense teaching you chemistry if you haven't learned your ABCs!

Think of Part 1 as kindergarten for needlecrafts. Passing it up will only set you back in school! In this section you'll pick up needlecraft history (always good for cocktail party gab), understand the differences between different types of needlecrafts, and learn some design basics. Pass the basics first, and then move up a grade to get stitching!

Chapter 1

An Ancient Craft with Modern Appeal

In This Chapter

➤ Learning the basics of your new craft

➤ Discovering the history of needlework

➤ Furnishing your home and spicing up your wardrobe with practical and pretty needlework

➤ Creating needlework as art

Recently, we've seen a resurgence of crafts—perhaps this is due to our desire to return to a simpler time, or the need to fill our lives with more personal items. TV personalities like Martha Stewart and Rosie O'Donnell have lent their cachet to crafts and handwork, making them popular and fashionable. From ornament painting to twig sculptures, everyone and her neighbor is filling her leisure time with an enjoyable craft.

And needlework is certainly part of this. Needlework, as your great, great, and even greater grandmother could have told you, has roots in a time when it was used for utilitarian as well as artistic purposes. However, with the advent of the Industrial Revolution and, more recently, with the invention of the computer, needlework's popularity went into a decline. But now, a renewed interest in anything handmade is causing a huge comeback. The ability to create useful and beautiful designs for your cousin's wedding gift, your daughter's wardrobe, or your own home makes needlework a truly satisfying craft. Needlework projects today can be as simple as a single letter monogram on a bath towel or an intricate wall hanging of museum quality.

Get Hooked on the Basics

In this book, we will explore the world of embroidery and needlepoint (which is actually a form of embroidery), two satisfying and creative forms of needlework. You will learn the basic stitches of embroidery: flat, crossed, and looped; as well as those of needlepoint: tent, diagonal, and straight—plus many more! Each needle art uses particular threads and yarns with appropriate needles and fabric. Producing good needlework goes hand in hand with having the right tools. Both embroidery and needlepoint create beautiful items to use, decorate with, and wear—quite a change from the utilitarian uses of earlier centuries.

The History of Needlework

Most of the needlework pieces from centuries ago have perished over time. Some of the more valuable needlework items, such as those sewn with expensive gold and silver threads and embellished with jewels, were stolen and unraveled by thieves. Although many of those pieces are gone forever, we can still study needlework from paintings that have been preserved and from surviving needlework samples. Wills, estate inventories from royal households, diaries, and other old documents contain accounts of the needlework created in times past, and these items further increase our knowledge of needlework history.

Clever Crafter

Since ancient embroideries are extremely scarce, we know of them from literature and other old documents. This fourth-century account from a bishop's sermon to his parishioners shows that needlework was alive and practiced:

> "Strive to follow in your lives the teachings of the Gospel rather than the miracles of our Redeemer embroidered upon your outward dress."

> —St. Asterius of Amasia

Embroidery

Embroidery is the art of embellishing a fabric with stitches to add beauty, depict a story, educate children, or record a special event. Historically, the thinnest of muslins to the heaviest and most pliable leathers were used. Luxurious threads and yarns like gold and cashmere were used to stitch some fabulous garments and household items.

Most countries used embroidery as a symbolic language as well as for decorative purposes. The Greeks and Romans bordered their tunics and togas in geometric patterns, oftentimes in gold thread to distinguish wealth and position. In China, embroidered butterflies were symbols of flirtation, bats of longevity, and geese of domestic happiness. The phoenix equaled beauty and good fortune but was reserved for the empress only. In India, embroidery was dictated by a code of strict rules handed down from generation to generation.

Varieties of Style and Purpose

In England needlework was primarily used for religious purposes. These pieces were considered precious because of their designs, not the quality of their threads, and are still held in high regard today. Medieval Germany embroiderers used beads and glass, linen *grounds,* and linen threads for their needlework instead of jewels and silks. The use of these humble materials sparked such new types of embroidery as beadwork, whitework, and openwork.

Italy became famous for openwork, a type of embroidery that is used to decorate linens with a "pulled thread method." Each stitch pulls the fabric threads together, creating open, lace-like patterns. This developed into needlepoint lace and a new technique called *voiding* in which the outlines of a design are filled in with long stitches and the interior is left unworked.

In sixteenth-century Spain, gold and jewels were stitched on scenes that had been painted on linen fabric. At the same time, *blackwork,* a type of embroidery in which black silk is stitched on white linen in swirling patterns, became popular. It is still used on garments today.

Needlework 101

Tapestry is a heavy, decorative woven fabric with a pictorial design that is worked in a needlepoint method.

Clever Crafter

In the eleventh century, France produced an epic embroidery known as the Bayeux Tapestry. It is 227 feet wide by 20 inches high, stitched in wool on linen, and depicts the 1066 battle in which William of Normandy defeated Harold, the Saxon pretender, to become king of England. That's one old heirloom!

Make Way for the Practical

In the seventeenth century, bejeweled and extravagant embroideries gave way to utilitarian works—bed hangings were embroidered with wool to help keep out drafts, and chairs were upholstered for the first time. Women tried to use their needlework expertise to make the home more comfortable. They couldn't hop in their SUV and head to K-Mart for Martha Stewart sheets. Needlework was not a hobby in early America —it provided basic home wares that were useful for everyday life.

In the eighteenth century, embroidery was used more and more on clothing, for both men and women.

Man vs. the Machine

By the nineteenth century, mass-produced needlework designs were available, along with needlework magazines. The influx of machine-made designs caused a decline in handmade work. *Berlinwork,* a needlepoint style originating in Germany, was popular in America.

The Twentieth Century

The twentieth century brought an awareness of tribal art from Africa and North American Indians. Regional embroidery around the world still flourished, and French couturiers employed fantastic designs using sequins, silver, and gold. Today, many French clothing designers still use the same techniques as their predecessors and look to these early innovators for inspiration.

Keeping It Alive Today

Needlework has made a big comeback with today's children who have grown up in the computer age. Parents, concerned that typing on a keyboard is their children's only form of creativity, want their kids to learn crafts, and needlework is an appealing, easy-to-learn craft. When children acquire this new skill, they keep the craft alive.

As our lives become increasingly high-tech, we cherish handcrafted items more and more, and we experience the calming powers of needlework in a hectic world. Needlework is a powerhouse in the world of crafts, both as a business and as a hobby, because handmade items and gifts never go out of style.

Pretty and Useful

Needlework is a beautiful way to embellish garments and home furnishings. Just about any item in your home can be created or spruced up with needlework. As a craft, needlework also establishes the good habit of finishing a project and it provides a unique way to express yourself. Creating your own design on a fancy tablecloth or on throw pillows that can be used for generations makes this practical craft uniquely personal. Needlepoint and embroidery also make a great companion; use your new craft to pass the time on a long ride or while listening to the evening news on television. Needlework offers the opportunity for you to take pride in something handmade and to give uniqueness to your home.

Ordinary dishtowels can be made special with a simple cross-stitched initial. Bed linens can be personalized with monograms and designs, and a needlepointed firescreen can add a decorative element to any room—no fireplace required—as will upholstered needlepoint stools and chair seats.

Some items you may not even think to embroider or needlepoint are a cocktail purse, brickcover doorstop, a belt, eyeglass case, or holiday ornaments.

Needlework 101

Turkeywork is a needlepoint term, invented in the sixteenth century, for stitches that resemble the pile of Turkish carpets.

Clever Crafter

Needlepoint was influenced by the Art Nouveau period at the end of the nineteenth century. William Morris of England introduced lilies instead of roses and soft blues and greens with Pre-Raphaelite figures.

Modern Uses at Home … Not Just for Toaster Covers!

Do you have one of those annoyingly crafty neighbors? You know, the kind who can turn a twig and some dental floss into a wing-backed chair. Well, you know what they say: If you can't beat them, join them. I can't promise that you'll be able to create furniture out of yarn, but needlework is a great way to turn your home into one that is envied by the neighbors.

Needlework has come a long way from its utilitarian purposes of mending, joining, and labeling. Today needleworked pieces can be framed as artwork in your home. Stitch a child's birth date or a couple's wedding date so that the special occasion is remembered forever. Reupholster the dining room chairs. Monogram your bed, bath, and kitchen linens. Stitch your favorite saying or a decorative motif on a pillow. All of these pieces add up to a one-of-a-kind home decor.

Expand Your Wardrobe

With so many mass-merchandised stores, there is a glut of cookie-cutter clothes on the market. Spruce up some jeans with embroidered designs on the bottoms or pockets. Use fancy stitches to add patches. Monogram a love note on the bottom of your favorite shirt. Needlepoint a handbag in your favorite colors, or add jewels to an evening cocktail bag. Document your life on a needlepoint belt with dates and motifs. Embroider a motif on a knit sweater (that's adding one type of needlework—embroidery—on top of another—knitting). The possibilities are endless!

Just for Show: Needlecraft as Art

If you become a needlework addict and feel competitive, you could enter your work in juried shows. These shows judge the quality of the piece's design, work, color, and overall effect. They are a good learning experience because you will learn how your work compares with others. In addition, you will be able to view the work of needlework artists who use their needles, yarns, and threads as their medium to create artistically prepared works of museum quality.

Some museums have areas that feature a wing devoted to the decorative arts. You can see beautiful examples of needlework that are truly art and get good ideas for designs, scaling their size or detail to your purposes. Chapter 8, "Designing Your Own Embroidery," examines this facet of embroidery in depth.

If you plan to eventually turn your hobby into extra income, opportunities await at a gazillion craft shows scattered all over the country. Check out Chapter 20, "More Than a Hobby," for further information on showing and selling your work.

The Least You Need to Know

➤ Needlework has roots in ancient times, where it was used to depict stories, religious themes, battles, and social standing.

➤ Embroidery is the art of decorating various fabrics with stitches for the purpose of beauty and decoration. Needlepoint is a form of embroidery.

➤ You can create useful things for your home and your wardrobe that are also unique.

➤ Embroidered garments and home furnishings reveal great personal style.

Well-Designed Needle Art

When you visit cousin Ted, do you cringe at the velvet Elvis paintings that cover his walls? Just remember: Elvis may not be your bag but it works for him. The same is true for needlecrafts. What works for someone else doesn't have to suit you. Use this beginner time to find your personal style and to understand what is most appealing to you.

Regardless of style, make sure you start out small. If a design of the *Mona Lisa* looks challenging, that's because it is! Stay away from choosing a big project for your first few attempts. Not being able to complete a project will only frustrate you and might keep you away from needlework forever.

Keeping in mind these tips, plus the basics of design, will allow you to make better choices when selecting the colors and patterns that float your boat.

Embroidery vs. Needlepoint: What's the Difference?

Embroidery is the art of decorating a background fabric with different stitches to add beauty. *Needlepoint* is a form of embroidery and is often worked with thicker yarns. Embroidery tends to use finer threads and is often found on delicate items such as handkerchiefs, blouses, and table linens, whereas needlepoint is usually used for items that receive a lot of wear and tear, such as a chair cover or a handbag. Each art has particular stitches, but some are common to both.

Needlepoint is the strongest and hardest-wearing of all types of needlework because of its background fabric and tight stitching. It is worked with a thread and needle on a strong canvas or evenweave linen where there are the same amount of threads horizontally as vertically. Needlepoint is one of the oldest forms of embroidery.

Needlework 101

The difference between embroidery and needlepoint? **Embroidery** is the art of decorating various fabrics with stitches for the purpose of beauty and decoration. **Needlepoint** is a form of embroidery that uses primarily canvas for background fabric and is the strongest-wearing of all types of needlework.

Choosing the Right Design for You

Needlework projects can be geared to every level of crafter. The best way to start is to decide whether you want to try needlepoint first or embroidery.

Both types of needlework are available in kit form for all levels, from beginners to experts, and in every taste and budget. A predesigned kit from your local stitchery store is a good choice for a first project. The kit has the pattern already drawn on the canvas, along with premeasured colors of yarn, the right size needle, and directions. The bigger the canvas, the longer the project will take. For the first-time needleworker, I suggest choosing a medium-sized design with a few colors so that you can accomplish the project in a length of time that is gratifying.

Pick a subject that you love, such as a favorite flower, the family dog, or a simple scene. And be sure the colors of yarn are your favorite colors. Using colors you like is key to enjoying your hobby and will also motivate you to complete your project.

Needlework projects can be heirloom items. Choose a design that you would want to frame or make into a useful piece, such as a purse or pincushion. Selecting the design and colors can be a daunting task, but if you brush up on the key elements of good design, you will be a full-fledged needleworker in no time!

A Stitch in Time

Kits are perfect for the newcomer to needlework, and there are many for you to choose from. But be aware that mass-produced designs run the gamut from artistic to mediocre. Kits tend to look less personal because they are designed to appeal to a large market, but, on the positive side, the price can be right. Some kits are done by fabulously talented designers (that are a bit more expensive), featuring spectacular patterns and fine yarn and color coordination. Of course, these kits are handsome when finished, but much more expensive. If your budget dictates what you can buy, then shop around for sales and other good deals—they are out there!

Design Basics

When selecting a needlework project, be sure to consider the elements of design: color, balance, scale, and texture. Just as with any artistic endeavor, all the parts add up to the final look of your finished project.

Clever Crafter

Take your new craft along for the ride. I once went on a year-long sailing trip. I took a huge bag of yarns left over from various needlework projects and fresh new canvases. I determined my own colors for all my needlework patterns using the yarns that I had, instead of using the preset colors on the canvases. I fashioned two pillows, a marriage sampler, a brick cover, and a framed piece. Now that was careful color coordination!

You might choose a project by the colors that you like. If you like reds and blues, you might want to stitch an American flag. Greens and blues? A sea scene from the coast of Maine. Browns and ivories? Your Springer Spaniel! You might pick out a project because it matches your wallpaper or because it reminds you of your grandmother's quilt.

Whichever project you decide on, once you learn the basics of design and color your own tastes will emerge. Before you know it, your needlework choices will become heirloom pieces!

Choosing Color: A Needleworker's Powerful Tool

Just as a first-time homeowner agonizes over room colors, a beginner needleworker may fuss over colors. Even if the yarns are prepackaged!

At first you may think that choosing colors is the easy part—after all, you have made color choices all of your life in clothing, flowers, and even your hair! Yet it is the lasting power of needlework that makes one fret over a few balls of yarn. Even a professional needleworker will get in a dither about what colors to select for a pillow, to say nothing of an enormous tapestry! You want the colors to be right if you are going to invest time and money in a piece, and you want to be pleased with the finished product.

Simple Science of Color

In case you've forgotten what you learned in your high school natural science course, I'll give you a quick refresher. What you see as a rainbow is actually sunlight passing through a prism. This progression of colors as wavelengths of light is often displayed as a "rainbow in the round" or a color wheel. The color wheel is an essential tool used by designers to create successful color schemes in needlework. The color wheel is broken down into 12 basic colors, with 3 *primaries,* 3 *secondaries,* and 6 *tertiaries.* By graphically showing how colors are related to each other, a color wheel can help you make sense of the endless possibilities of color combinations. Studying the color wheel and learning the language of color will help you gain confidence as you enter the realm of the rainbow. See the color section in the middle of the book for your color wheel guide.

Here's a chance for you to brush up on the international language of color—your eighth-grade art teacher would be so proud!

➤ **Primary colors** are red, blue, and yellow. These are the pure hues that all other colors are derived from. They are not mixed from any other colors. They are spaced equidistant from one another on the color wheel.

➤ **Secondary colors** are orange, green, and violet. They are the three colors mixed from equal amounts of two primary colors. (Red + yellow = orange; yellow + blue = green; red + blue = violet.)

A Stitch in Time

The associations you make with different colors are based on your personality, your everyday experiences, your past, and the world you live in. Your personal color choices can profoundly affect your response to artwork, home interiors, and needlework. Many color associations are based on common social conventions and gender associations, such as dressing girls in pink. The way you perceive certain colors will influence which colors you use when selecting yarns and kits.

➤ **Tertiary colors** are the six colors produced by mixing a primary with its adjacent secondary. For example: red + orange = orange-red; red + purple = red-purple … and so on.

➤ **Complementary colors** are colors directly opposite each other on the color wheel. For example: red and green, blue and orange, yellow and violet.

➤ **Harmonies** are closely related colors that lie between two primaries on the color wheel, such as blue-violet and violet.

➤ **Hue** is an identifying color, such as apple green, sea green, or hunter green.

➤ **Tone** defines the lightness or darkness of a color.

➤ **Tint** is a color's range from a pure hue to white, such as red to pink to white. Tints are considered light tones.

➤ **Shade** is a color's range from a pure hue to black, such as yellow to deep gold to black. Shades are considered dark tones.

The color wheel provides reliable and fascinating ways to explore color schemes. You can either link color families or take advantage of their contrasting qualities. A simple approach is to use a monochromatic color scheme with one hue in various tints and shades and enough contrast so as not to appear dull.

A Stitch in Time

The fibers of a yarn affect its color. Two yarns, each made of a different fiber but both having the same shade, will look quite dissimilar, even though the shades are the same. A wool, a floss, a pearl cotton, and a matte cotton will all appear different because each absorbs light differently.

Clever Crafter

Did you know that color can affect your mood? Sunny colors such as red, yellow, and orange can enliven your soul or stir your fiery passion! On the other hand, blues, greens, and purples turn down the visual heat and your mood.

Using a single-color yarn with some tints and shades makes a monochromatic needlepoint anything but boring. In fact, shading adds depth and interest, and changes in texture and stitching can make the same color look dramatically different.

Color Your World

The best way to learn how to combine colors is to observe. Noting great combinations, whether in a fashion magazine, in a walk through the woods, or in inspiring artwork, will help when choosing colors for your needlework.

Remember the colors that catch your eye the most. For more ideas, go through your wardrobe to see whether there is a particular piece of clothing that you could translate to your needlework, possibly a scarf or a tie. Flowers in a garden may draw your attention with their harmonious arrangement, or a photograph from a family vacation might just get your creative juices flowing. A tour through a friend's home that you admire is also a good way to study color.

If you're really stumped about which colors to choose, select yarn or kit colors that resemble something you love: fabric from a drape, a favorite painting, or even another needlework. The color combination in these objects can guide you to a scheme for one or more needlework projects.

Decorator's Do's and Don'ts

Don't always choose typical combinations of threads and fabrics. All of your projects will tend to look the same. Artistic pairings of rough and refined fabrics, such as denim and chenille, burlap and silk, often make for interesting needlework.

Getting a Feel for Texture

Flat is fine if your hobby is, say, leaf pressing, but needlework is a hands-on craft in every way. Without texture, a needlework piece would be without depth and character. Texture will encourage an admirer to touch your piece and really appreciate the variety of stitches and the intricacies of your hard work.

Just as color stimulates emotion, so does texture. For example, needlepoint textures can be smooth, soft, and warm, or rough, hard, and cold. The visual and tactile impact that texture plays is considered in the pattern on your ground, the colors chosen, the stitches planned, and the yarn fibers. Texture and color go hand in hand when planning a design. A yellow yarn in wool in a satin stitch will look totally different from a yellow yarn in matte cotton in the same stitch.

Bringing It Together

If color and texture can be thought of as the raw ingredients of design, then proportion and balance are the binding agents that complete the recipe for successful needlework design.

Proportionally Speaking

Having good *proportion* in your design means that the size and shape of a part match the whole piece. For example, the size of a piece of fruit should be in relation to the size of its basket, or the nearness of a person to a mountain in the background should be appropriate to the perspective of the entire scene.

It All Hangs in the Balance

Balance appeals to our sense of equilibrium, a visual "weight." Balancing patterns, textures, colors, and emotions in your needlework creates harmony of design.

You can achieve *symmetrical balance* by arranging the same designs on each side of a center or dominant pattern. Little imagination is required to do this, and your visual sense of symmetry allows you to easily understand the concept.

Asymmetrical balance is achieved by arranging equal visual weights that are not identical, such as two children on one side of a home and an adult on the other side. Although their actual weight may not be the same, their visual weights are balanced.

Clever Crafter

Always remember: Proportions and "weights" of yarns, stitches, and patterns all play a significant role in the total impact of your needlework design.

You've Got Style: Use It!

Personal style is a unique blend of tastes and preferences that you have acquired and shaped over your lifetime. It is inspired by the home that you grew up in, the places you have visited, the people you have met, and just about everything else that you have experienced: music and museums, books and movies, gardens and garage sales. Let your style come through when you select a pattern, add a fringe or ruffle to your finished work, or embellish the corners of pillows with tassels. Your style can make an ordinary needlework a work of art!

A Stitch in Time

Always carry a notepad to record interesting patterns or color combinations that you might see while attending a movie, a museum, or a home tour, or while shopping at a fabric store.

Gain confidence in your personal style through reading and critiquing, exposure and observation. Start perusing art and antique magazines, home and interior books, and needlework pattern books. Be on the lookout for ideas from unusual places or objects: Perhaps a silk scarf or a bouquet of flowers has all of the right color combinations for a needlepoint footstool. Mail-order catalogs may have interesting pictures of needle-worked home furnishings. See Appendix A, "Resources for Novice Needleworkers," to help you define your tastes.

The Least You Need to Know

➤ Choose a needlework design that fits your skill level and personal style.

➤ Color and texture are key elements of any needlework design.

➤ Balance and proportion complete well-designed needlework.

➤ Incorporating personal style into your needlework adds uniqueness to any project.

Part 2

Embroidery Basics

Spending some quality time in Part 2 will give you a great head start in learning embroidery. I've packed these chapters with all the basic info you'll need to dive right into your first embroidery project. You'll learn about the tools you need, several different stitch techniques, and ways to make your projects unique. Soak up these chapters as best you can, and then start stitching away!

Chapter 3

Tools of
the Trade

In This Chapter

➤ Choosing the perfect background

➤ Learning the basic types of needles and threads

➤ Keeping it all together with frames

➤ Starting with a beginner kit

With your new design and color sense, and a feeling of what style will work for you, you are ready to get to work. But, like any good craftsperson, you will need the right tools before you start stitching away. As a novice embroiderer, it's important to learn about needle size, appropriate fabrics, frames, and thread types, as well as the kinds of kits that are available. The beauty of embroidery is the harmony created with the pairing of canvas and threads, the correct gauge needles and stitches, and the design for the project at hand.

The Material World of Embroidery

There is quite a range of background fabrics available for any embroidery project. Actually, any fabric can be embroidered as long as it is firm enough to hold stitches, supple enough to allow a needle to pass in and out of, and wear-resistant enough to hold up during stitching. Most embroidery fabrics range from fine silks to thick wools. Solid fabrics are the norm, but printed and patterned fabrics can be used as a design guide, following the print with your needle and thread.

Woven fabrics work well, too. A wide range of *evenweave* fabrics are available for *counted thread techniques,* which rely on counting the threads of the fabric to achieve

Needlework 101

Evenweave is a type of fabric that has the same number of warp threads (the threads that go up and down) as it has weft threads (the ones that go side to side) per square inch. For example, an 18-count evenweave fabric has 18 threads to the inch, both vertically and horizontally.

the pattern. The four types of natural fabrics most commonly used for embroidery are cottons, silks, linens, and wools.

A very popular embroidery cloth is 14-count Aida cloth. This versatile cotton fabric is available in a wide range of colors and is suitable for many types of threads and designs. Stitching is enjoyable because your needle and thread can be easily brought in and out of the fabric. Aida is woven in a design that looks like little squares, making it easy to place one stitch in each square and to count spaces. This fabric is also available with a colored grid to make stitch counting from a chart easier and is thus a good choice for beginners. The colored threads are removed when the stitching is done. Fourteen-count Aida cloth is readily available at stitchery shops and craft stores. Aida also comes in other thread counts, including 11-count for tired eyes and 18-count for more delicate effects.

Evenweave fabrics are a good choice for counted thread techniques such as cross stitch.

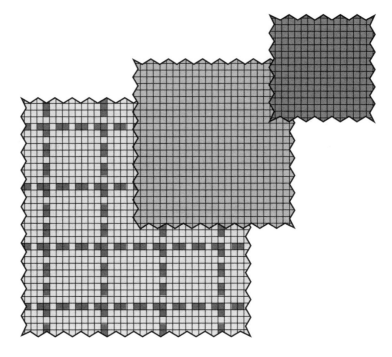

Nice Threads!

Threads come in an exciting range of colors and fibers. Some popular fibers used for threads are silks, cottons, linens, wools, metals, and synthetics. Particular weights and thickness of threads are suited for certain types of background fabrics. You can also experiment with other yarns, such as those made for knitting or crochet. Familiarize yourself with the following embroidery threads and examples of backgrounds that can be used with each:

➤ **Embroidery floss.** A loosely twisted six-strand cotton thread that is easily divided into single threads. Works well on linen or cotton fabrics.

➤ **Matte embroidery thread.** A thick, soft, tightly twisted thread. Works well on evenweave fabrics in linen and cotton.

➤ **Crewel yarn.** A fine two-*ply* wool or acrylic yarn. Works well on linen.

➤ **Flower thread.** A fine thread that cannot be divided and has a matte finish. Works well on tightly woven fabrics and cottons and linens.

➤ **Pearl cotton.** A strong, twisted thread that cannot be divided and has a high sheen. Works well on cottons, linens, and wools.

➤ **Persian yarn.** Loosely twisted three-strand wool or acrylic yarn that is easily divided. Works well on cottons, wools, and linens.

Needlework 101

Ply is a component of a strand of thread or yarn. Plies make up the strand and strands make up the thread or yarn. For example, if you remove one strand from a six-strand floss and untwist the strand, you will see that the single strand is composed of two plies.

The best way to choose yarn, if it is not already prepackaged in a kit, is to assess the look that you want for your design and the type of fabric you are using. Fine threads will look neat on delicate fabrics, whereas woolly threads will be bulkier-looking and may require a rougher, heavier fabric. But sometimes the most creative looks come when you match rough with refined—you know, opposites attract … silk thread on wool and wool thread on silk fabric. The most important thing to keep in mind when you buy your thread is its weight and thickness. If it's too heavy, it will distort the fabric that you are working on; too flimsy and you will not be able to see your stitching. Experiment with different threads and fabrics, and you can come up with some clever combinations.

The Fine Points of Needles

Embroidery needles are made in a range of sizes, usually in categories classified by the type of work or fabric they are designed for. Fine-gauge needles, which are small and thin, are for finer cloths or grounds, and larger-gauge needles are used for coarser grounds.

A good rule of thumb to remember is that the finer the needle, the higher the number. Usually the eye of the needle is long to make threading it easier. One exception is the needle used for metal work. The eye is round in order to hold the thread in place so that it will not slide within the eye. This protects the rest of the thread, outside the eye, from the abrasion of being pulled through the eye.

Types of needles: crewel, chenille, tapestry, and beading.

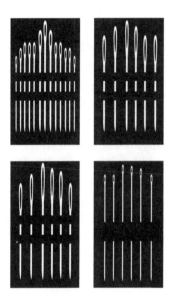

You may have already guessed that different types of embroidery work require different needles. Some of the most common embroidery needles are:

➤ **Crewel or embroidery needle.** This is the most commonly used needle. It has a sharp point and large eye that is used for crewel work.

➤ **Chenille needle.** Similar to a crewel needle but with a thicker shaft. The chenille needle is good for heavy threads and coarse grounds.

➤ **Tapestry needle.** A thick-shafted, large-eyed needle with a round-pointed end; the tapestry (or yarn) needle works best for evenweave fabrics because it is designed to slip between the threads rather than to pierce them as a crewel needle does.

➤ **Beading needle.** A fine, long needle with a tiny eye used for sewing small beads.

Clever Crafter

The first needles were made of thorns and fish bones!

Taut and Tidy Frames

Embroidery frames are used to hold the ground fabric taut so the embroiderer can concentrate on the task at hand. Small projects may not necessarily need a frame, but a frame helps to make the work easier to handle and quicker to stitch. It also helps to hold the fabric permanently taut and evenly stretched to ensure even stitches. Your work stays cleaner with a frame because it is handled less. Also, a frame on a stand allows your hands to be free to work the stitches. Two basic types of frames are round (hoop frame) and straight-sided.

The *hoop frame* is most popular because it is portable, lightweight, and easy to mount. It can be made of wood, plastic, or metal, and it ranges in sizes from 5 to 10 inches in diameter. The frame is composed of two hoops that are placed one inside the other, stretching the fabric between them. The outer hoop has an opening in it and a screw to adjust the tension.

The *straight-sided frame* (also known as a stretcher frame) has a roller top and bottom and is usually used for larger wall hangings but is suitable for all types of embroidery. A straight frame stretches the fabric very evenly and allows for a large part of the work to be visible (good for freehand design). Although more time is needed to mount a piece on a straight-sided frame, the piece is quickly moved into a new position as your stitching progresses. There are the latest Q-snap frames made of PVC pipe. Not only are they inexpensive, available in many sizes, and a "snap" to use, but they provide excellent tension and do not crease the fabric—which is the chief drawback of hoops. For many people they have replaced roller frames because there is no tedious mounting process. They work well for small and medium-size projects.

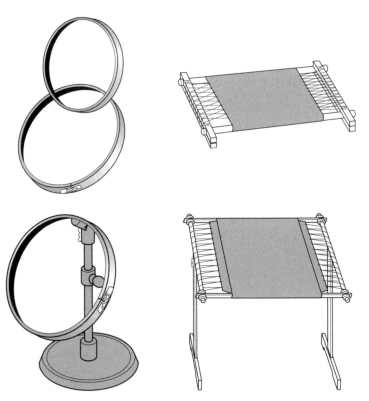

Types of frames: hoop, straight-sided, hoop on stand, and straight-sided on stand.

Both types of frames are available as floor or lap stands, which allow both hands to be free. The hoop frame is easily portable, so I often carry this type when I am stitching small projects on the go. At home, I love my frames on stands for larger projects, such as a wall hanging. The stand is always set up, and I can work on it at different times throughout the day.

Little Extras Make a Big Difference

Good results in embroidery come from using good-quality implements. Along with the right needles and threads, fill your embroiderer's basket with the following:

➤ **Embroidery scissors.** Find a pair that is sharp, light, and pointed.

➤ **Dressmaker shears.** Use for cutting fabric.

➤ **Thimble.** Protect your fingertips. A good thimble should have well-defined indentations.

➤ **Pincushion.** Use it to corral pins and needles and protect them from rust.

➤ **Embroidery marker.** Try this for drawing designs on fabric.

➤ **Embroidery transfer pencil.** Use for hot-iron transfer designs.

➤ **Needle threader.** Make threading a needle easier.

➤ **Masking tape.** Use to bind edges of fabric to prevent raveling.

➤ **Dressmaker's carbon paper.** Use to transfer designs to fabric.

➤ **Magnifiers.** Used to aid in the magnification of the work at hand. Some are available in the form of eyeglasses or a stand, both allowing your hands to be free.

Kits: Packaged Goods

As I mentioned in Chapter 2, "Well-Designed Needle Art," most beginner needleworkers start with a kit. Embroidery kits are prepackaged and contain ground cloth, a needle, embroidery floss, and directions. Kits have predetermined designs and colors of yarn and come in all levels of difficulties, prices, and tastes. Some kits are designed by professional needlework designers, and these are usually more expensive and available at specialty needlework stores or through catalogs. Others are manufactured by commercial companies that cater to every taste and budget and are available at local

Decorator's Do's and Don'ts

Don't be in the dark! Set up your embroidery stand in a well-lit area. It should be under direct lighting or at least a directed spotlight. Good lighting is essential for working embroidery. It protects your eyes and helps you to differentiate between different color tones of yarn and pattern.

chain stores in the craft section or at craft stores. Basic cross stitch is probably the most popular because it is quick and easy to master. You will learn how to cross-stitch in Chapter 5, "In Stitches." See Appendix A, "Resources for Novice Needleworkers," for resources for embroidery kits.

The Least You Need to Know

➤ Any fabric can be embroidered as long as it is firm enough to hold stitches and supple enough to allow a needle to pass through.

➤ Particular weights and thicknesses of threads are suited for different ground cloths.

➤ Different needles are used for different types of embroidery and grounds.

➤ Embroidery frames hold your cloth permanently taut and are available in hoop or straight style.

➤ Embroidery kits are a good option for a beginner needleworker.

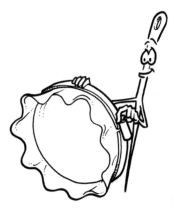

Chapter 4

Technique Chic

In This Chapter

➤ Preparing tight and tidy frames

➤ Setting up your fabric and threads

➤ Improving your look with basic techniques and tips

➤ Getting the designs you want with enlarging, reducing, and transferring techniques

---

Before you're ready to dive into your first embroidery project (almost there!), you need to learn some basic techniques on how to prepare your frame, fabric, and threads.

If you choose to create your own design, you will need to review the techniques of enlarging, reducing, and transferring. You'll also learn some tricks of the trade, such as the best way to prepare certain types of thread and fabric.

And how about inspiration for designs? Get some tips in this chapter and refer back to the paragraph on personal style in Chapter 2, "Well-Designed Needle Art."

Needlework preparation is like starting your day with a good breakfast. Correctly preparing your project before you start will help you concentrate on your design, just as a nutritious breakfast starts your day off right. Now, grab a bowl full of fabric and thread, and let's get to work!

Consider Yourself Framed!

In Chapter 3, "Tools of the Trade," you learned about round (hoop) and straight-sided frames that can be used to hold your project in place while you work. Lightweight hoop frames are suitable for small pieces of fabric, and straight-sided frames are good choices for larger pieces. The hoop is fairly easy to mount. The straight-sided frame takes a little longer to put together because the fabric needs to be affixed to the frame. Both are available on floor or lap stands that allow you to keep both hands free.

Setting Up the Hoop Frame

Before placing the fabric in the hoop frame, loosen the tension screw on the outer hoop. Lay the fabric on the inner hoop with the section to be embroidered facing you. Always keep the fabric smooth. Place the outer hoop down on top of the inner hoop, keeping the fabric correctly positioned. Press gently and pull fabric taut. Tighten the outer hoop screw to hold the fabric firmly into position, as shown in the next figure.

Fabric in a hoop frame should be drum-tight.

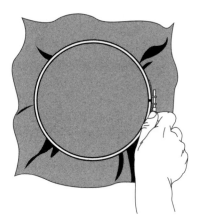

Mounting Odd Shapes

You may find yourself with pieces that are too small or irregularly shaped to fit into your frame. To embroider them, you'll need to *baste* these small or odd pieces to a larger piece of fabric. To baste, simply sew the smaller piece on top of the larger one, using large stitches. You can then mount the entire piece into a frame. When the piece is firmly in place, cut away the supporting fabric underneath the design, leaving your design ready for embroidering, as shown here.

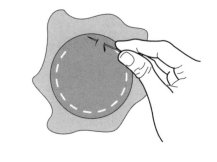

Mount the fabric in the usual way after you have basted the smaller fabric onto the larger piece.

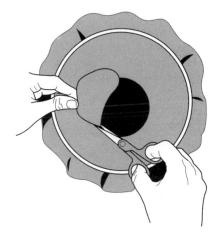

When cutting away your supporting fabric, take extra care to avoid nipping your design!

Binding the Frame

Sometimes, fine embroidery fabrics such as silk or satin can sag in the frame while you are working on it. To correct this, you will need to bind the inner hoop with woven tape as shown in the following figure. Stitch the ends of the binding tape together. This will also prevent your fabric from shifting in the frame.

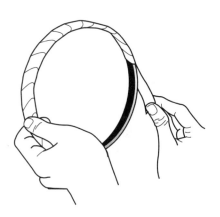

Be sure to fasten the ends of the woven tape with a few stitches while binding the frame.

31

Clever Crafter

Old, unfinished needlework stretched on a large straight-sided frame can be hung as artwork on a wall in your home!

Preparing the Straight-Sided Frame

Straight-sided frames are a little more complicated to mount and disassemble because the top and bottom of the fabric are sewn on the roller webbing and the sides need to be laced to the frame.

Before you begin, hem all of the edges of your fabric or bind them with ¾-inch wide cotton tape. Mark a center point on both the top and bottom edges. As pictured, match the center points of fabric with center points of rollers on the frame. Stitch the fabric to the roller webbing, starting from the center and working outward as shown in the following figure.

Be sure to mark the center of the rollers and the top and bottom of the fabric when stitching the fabric to the roller webbing.

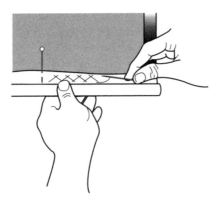

Next, slot the sides into the rollers and pull taut by adjusting screws or pegs. As shown in the following figure, lace the sides of the fabric to the sides of the frame with strong thread such as button thread (thread that is specifically used for sewing on buttons because of its strength). Lace sides loosely at first but then tighten them alternately, getting an equal pull on both sides. Adjust the fabric at the top as well and keep making adjustments until the fabric is evenly taut and secure with firm knots.

It is essential to get an even stretch across the entire surface of the fabric. Adjustment of the lacing and rollers may be necessary.

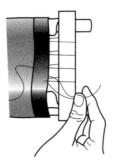

The Nitty-Gritty Basics

Now that you know how to prepare a frame, you're ready to prepare your fabric and threads and learn some basic techniques to start and finish your work.

Cutting and Binding

If you choose to use your own fabric and not a kit, cut your fabric two inches larger than the overall design. If you plan to frame your completed embroidery, add four inches to the overall pattern. For example, if your finished design is 6 inches by 6 inches and you want to frame it, cut your cloth 14 inches by 14 inches. Cut your fabric with care—use straight lines and try to follow the warp and weft threads of the fabric's weave.

Binding your embroidery fabric prevents the edges from fraying while you work, especially if your fabric is loosely woven. Three popular choices are to machine zigzag the outer edge of your cloth, to turn under the edges and hand-sew in place, or to tape the outer edge with masking tape. If your sewing machine has a serger (a feature that binds the edges of fabric with threads close together),then you can serge the outer edges.

Preparing the Threads

The *working thread,* which is the thread you are using, should be 18 inches or less. Any longer and the thread will become tangled, will fray, or will lose its sheen.

Embroidery floss, matte embroidery cotton, and Persian yarn are all loosely twisted threads. These can be separated into finer threads for use, but wait until you are actually ready to work before separating them. This will prevent them from getting tangled before use.

A Stitch in Time

If you are stitching a large area in the same color, cut your threads or yarn to 18-inch lengths before you start. Fold threads into half bundles, tie with a loop end, and use as needed.

From Start to Finish

To secure a new working thread, turn your work to the backside, and slide your threaded needle through the underside of the previous stitches. Allow enough thread to leave a tail that is easily worked, say a half inch to an inch. Bring your needle up onto the right side of the fabric and continue with your design. See the following figure.

To secure your thread at the start of stitching, hold the end of the wrong side of the fabric and work stitches over the tail.

Starting a new thread in this manner ensures that there are no knots to cause a bumpy surface.

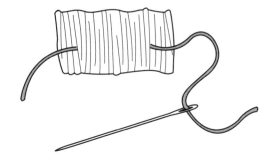

When you are ready to end your thread, again turn your work to the back, and slide the needle under 1½ inches of the worked stitches. Neatly cut the thread at the point where it emerges from the worked stitches. See the following figure.

When you are finished with a thread, be sure that you secure it on the wrong side of the fabric.

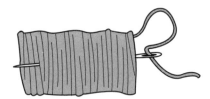

Knots in threads can show through your work. Don't make a knot when you are starting or finishing a length of thread. Either weave the end into the stitches on the back of your work or use a tiny back stitch (see the "Flat Stitches" section in Chapter 5, "In Stitches").

A Stitch in Time

When piercing your fabric with your needle, a stabbing motion works best. A clean hole is made in the fabric eliminating any damage to the surface of the fabric. Be sure to pull thread slowly and carefully.

Helpful Tips

Learning even the smallest tips and techniques used by the pros will help make your work look professional, too!

➤ Always use good light to avoid straining your eyes.

➤ Follow guidelines, the printed lines of the pattern on the cloth, carefully so they will not show in the finished design. Kits will usually have the printed design lines already on the cloth.

➤ Be sure to match your needle and thread in type and weight.

➤ Keep stitch tension even.

➤ Use a "stabbing motion" whenever possible for even tension when piercing the fabric.

➤ If your thread twists, let the needle fall freely and the thread will untwist itself.

➤ Choose shorter stitches if the item is to be handled or worn frequently. Shorter stitches hold up better, whereas longer stitches tend to snag and show wear more quickly.

Clever Crafter

Reuse plastic comforter covers with zippers to store your large embroidery projects!

Enlarging and Reducing Designs

The easiest way to enlarge a design is to use a photocopier that allows you to bring the design up to 200 percent. You can also take it to a professional copy store if you need it larger than that. A more time-consuming way to enlarge a design is the grid method, as shown in the following figure.

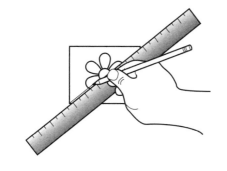

With a pencil, trace your pattern on tracing paper. Next, go over all of the lines with a black felt tip marker. Draw a rectangle around the new tracing. Draw a diagonal line from the bottom left corner to the top right corner.

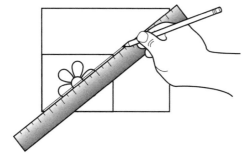

Place your traced rectangle in the bottom left corner of a sheet of paper ample enough for the size of your final design. Tape down the traced design, and extend your diagonal line from the tracing paper to across the larger paper.

Remove the tracing paper, and complete the diagonal line on the paper where the tracing used to be. At the top of your design on the tracing that you have just removed, use a triangle to draw a horizontal line to cross diagonally. From the point of intersection, draw a vertical line down to the bottom edge.

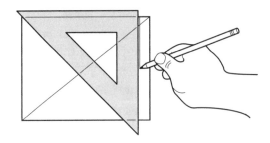

Now, draw equal-sized squares on the original tracing so that you have a grid. Draw the same number of squares onto the paper enlargement. Draw the lines of your design in each of the large squares on the paper, copying from the small squares on the tracing. Mark the points where the pattern lines intersect the grid, and join them together.

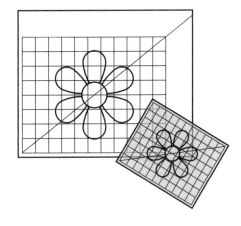

Decorator's Do's and Don'ts

Don't be afraid of ornate patterns and intricate designs. If a pattern you adore is very detailed, try to simplify the outline for your design and be sure to keep the scale in mind.

To reduce a design, making it smaller to fit your fabric, reverse the order of enlarging. Start with step 1, but place a small piece of paper on the tracing paper in the bottom left corner instead of a large one. Continue on with steps 3 and 4.

Transferring a Design

If you choose not to use a kit, how will you transfer your design to your fabric? There are several ways. The method that you choose will depend on the texture of the fabric and the type of design.

Freehand Embroidery

If you are already at ease with drawing and know some stitches, you can design a pattern as you are stitching. If you do not feel comfortable with free-hand stitching and you are artistically inclined, you can draw your pattern directly onto the fabric by using a pencil or embroidery marker, which is a fine tip marker that is water-soluble. Color in areas if you need an entire picture in front of you.

Tracing with Dressmaker's Carbon

Dressmaker's carbon works well on smooth fabrics. Use dark dressmaker's carbon for light fabrics and light dressmaker's carbon for dark fabrics. That way when you trace your pattern on the fabric, the outlines will show up better. Place the carbon between your drawing and the fabric with the drawing on top. Draw over the outlines. Remove the carbon and your design is ready to go!

Clever Crafter

Embroider your experiences in grid form. One square could be the state where you live; another could be your favorite hobby or the initials of your children or spouse, your dog Fluffy, etc.

If the fabric is sheer enough and you are comfortable with tracing, you can trace directly onto your fabric. Always test the carbon paper on a sample fabric before you draw directly on your embroidery cloth. Test to see if lines are able to be removed if you make a mistake or that the cloth will take the carbon lines.

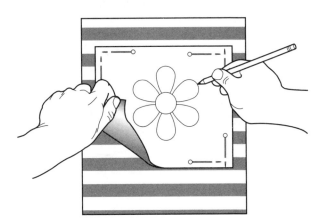

Be sure that you haven't missed any lines before you remove the design or carbon paper.

Hot Iron Transfer

Another way to transfer your design is to use a hot iron transfer. Begin by copying the design onto tracing paper. Turn the paper over, and trace the lines with an embroidery-transfer pencil. Place the paper with the marker-side down on your fabric, and pin together. With your iron on low heat, press over the pattern, applying pressure as you do so. Do not slide the iron back and forth because smudging may occur. Pull back a corner of the tracing paper to see if the pattern has been transferred. If so, remove the pins and the tracing.

Do not remove the transfer paper unless you have checked to make sure that the design is visible on the fabric.

Basting Through Tissue Paper

Basting a pattern onto tissue paper is a good method for coarse fabrics that might not take to the carbon very well. Trace your design on the tissue paper. Pin the tissue paper to your fabric, and baste the pattern through the tissue onto the fabric. Gently remove the tissue, leaving stitches in place on the fabric. After completing your embroidery, pull out any visible basting stitches with a pair of tweezers.

It is a good idea to choose a thread color that contrasts with your fabric. Then, when you remove the basting threads, the stitches are easily visible.

Tracing-Paper Templates

Using tracing-paper templates is a good method if you are embroidering simple shapes. You will need heavyweight tracing paper or clear acetate (which can be reused over and over). Draw your design onto the paper or acetate, and cut out each piece separately. Pin all shapes onto the fabric, and draw around them with your embroidery marker. If the fabric is coarse, baste around the templates instead. If repeating the design, re-pin the templates and redraw on next section.

Clever Crafter

A fast way to transfer a design? Use a rubber stamp with your favorite motif. Stamp onto your fabric and you're ready to begin!

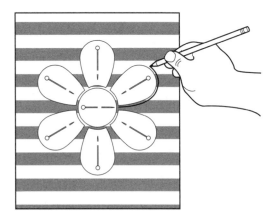

Clear acetate templates can be used over and over!

Clever Crafter

A fun way to trace a design from nature, say a leaf, is to lay a piece of firm but fine paper over the leaf, hold down the paper with one hand, and run a soft pencil back and forth over the paper and leaf. An impression of the leaf will appear. Remove the paper and draw around the embossed design. Trace and transfer!

The Least You Need to Know

➤ Frames help to keep your embroidery fabric taut to ensure even stitching. They also help to keep your project clean. Frames on stands allow both hands to be free.

➤ Learning basic techniques and tips will make your embroidery projects look professional!

➤ Patterns that you admire can be copied and embroidered by using various transfer techniques. By using the techniques of enlarging and reducing, you can suit any pattern to the size of your project.

Chapter 5

In Stitches

In This Chapter

➤ The basis of all sewing—the flat stitch

➤ The best-known embroidery stitch—the cross stitch

➤ The versatile looped stitch

➤ The textured knotted stitch

There are hundreds of stitches to use in embroidery. You can probably live an entire lifetime without even coming close to learning them all. Don't panic! You won't need to know every type of stitch before attempting the craft. Needleworkers around the world use many of the same stitches, some indigenous to their region, but all are variations from the four basic "food" groups of embroidery: flat, crossed, looped, and knotted.

At First Stitch

As a novice embroiderer, it might seem a little nerve-wracking to start a project that requires you to concentrate on everything at once: the design, the thread and fabric, the needle, the positioning of the fabric in the frame, and the stitching technique. Putting down that first stitch will be the toughest, but don't hesitate—pick up that needle and thread and get to work. And don't forget to enjoy your project as you do!

The following needlework tips are sure to keep you in stitches!

➤ Always work in good light so you can see your stitching!

➤ Keep your thread tangle-free by using a length of 18 inches or less as the working thread.

➤ Use blunt-tipped needles for cross stitch and sharp-tipped needles for all other embroidery. The needle should be small enough to enter the fabric easily without leaving an obvious hole but large enough not to fall through to the back of the fabric.

Flat Stitches

Flat stitches consist of straight surface stitches worked in different lengths and directions. They are referred to as flat stitches because they are not raised up from the fabric and tend to lie "flat" on the fabric. Flat stitches are the easiest to learn and some of the oldest stitches known. Types of flat stitches that you will learn are running, double running, back, stem, encroaching, split, straight, satin, and seed.

Running Stitch

The *running* stitch is the simplest of all the stitches. It is used for making lines, for outlining, and as a foundation for other stitches. On its own, as shown in the following figure, the running stitch looks like a broken line. The running and double running stitch are reversible—they appear the same on the back and front of the fabric.

To work the running stitch, take several small, neat stitches at one time. This is a stitch that uses a sewing motion.

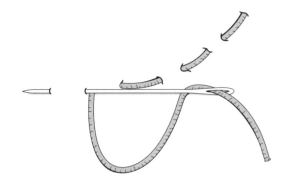

Double Running Stitch

The *double running* stitch is the leapfrog of all stitches, created by jumping under and over itself. First work a row of running stitches. Then start at the beginning of your first row and work a second row in between the stitches already laid down. You will be stitching in the same direction to fill in the gaps.

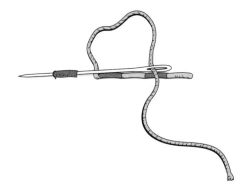

Use the same or a contrasting color for the second row of double running stitches.

Be sure to create a nice even line by moving the thread in and out of the thread holes created by the first row of running stitches. Use the double running stitch for both outlines and fillings.

Backstitch

The *backstitch* is worked in a straight line like the running stitch. The difference between the two is that backstitches are worked end-to-end and no spaces are left in between. To create the backstitch, first bring the needle to the front of the fabric at your starting point. Take a small backward stitch by placing the needle behind your starting point and bringing it down through the fabric and then up through the fabric in front of the starting point so there is space between your thread and the stitch you just made. Continue with the back and front pattern to create a neat line or outline.

A Stitch in Time

The double running stitch is also known as the Roumanian stitch or Holbein stitch.

Backstitches should be small and even, similar to machine stitching.

The backstitch, also known as the "point de sable" stitch, is more raised than the double running.

Stem Stitch

The *stem,* or "crewel," stitch is a principal embroidery stitch used for outlines, lines, grounds, fillings, and shading.

To begin, bring the needle to the front side of the fabric at the starting point. Pull the needle through to the front of the fabric halfway between your starting point and your first stitch. Create another full stitch next to the first one and continue working the stitches, raising the thread slightly above the previous stitch. Stem stitches are great for flowing or curvy lines. Work from left to right, keeping the stitch length consistent. On a corner or tight curves, make your stem stitches a bit shorter in order to create a smooth-looking line.

Stem stitches are slanted backstitches stitched side-by-side to look like rope.

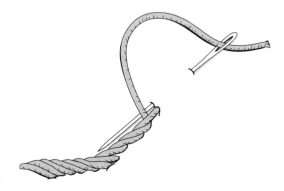

Straight Stitch

Straight stitches are single stitches that are spaced a little apart. Unlike running and double running stitches, straight stitches can vary in size. Bring your needle in and out of the fabric in single, spaced stitches.

Straight stitches are best when created short and close together. They are good for filling patterns or depicting things like grass or landscape items.

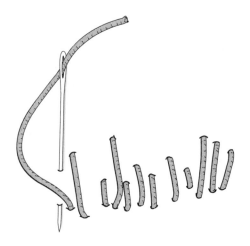

Satin Stitch

Satin stitches are straight stitches that are worked side by side to completely fill an area. Start at the widest section of your design. Bring the needle from the back of the fabric through to the front, coming up at the base of the stitch. Then go back down at the top of the stitch. Keep the satin stitches close together as you progress toward the narrower sections of the design.

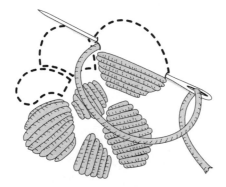

Although the satin stitch looks simple, its beauty lies in placing the stitches evenly and close together.

The satin stitch is used for outlining, filling, shaded effects, and geometric patterns. Try to keep your tension the same throughout so that the stitches lie smoothly, without looking too tight or too loose. Don't make the stitches too long. Long stitches can become loose and untidy.

Seed Stitch

Seed stitches are very small uniform stitches—hence the name "seed"—that are used to fill in an area. The seed stitch gives a more raised surface than the running stitch.

Make two side-by-side backstitches into the same holes, leaving a space between the next pair of stitches. The two stitches together give a stronger effect than a single seed stitch.

The seed stitch can be used to give a dotted effect.

Clever Crafter

When using the encroaching satin stitch, the tones can be changed in every row to produce a very subtle effect.

Encroaching Satin Stitch

The *encroaching satin* stitch is used for blending colors and providing soft tonal effects. I also like to use it to depict birds and animals.

For the first row, use the same technique as you would for the regular satin stitch described earlier. The second and subsequent rows are worked so that the head of the new stitch lies between the bases of the stitches in the first row, as in the following figure.

The encroaching satin stitch is used for blending colors and giving soft tonal effects.

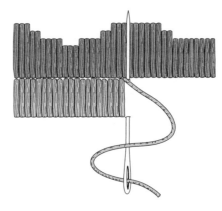

Crossed Stitches

The *cross* stitch is the best known, as well as one of the oldest and most popular, of all of the embroidery stitches. It's probably the stitch that you envision when thinking of embroidery. This stitch is quick and easy to master.

Basic Cross Stitch

The basic cross stitch is composed of two stitches, or "legs," that cross each other to form an X shape. The first stitch is a diagonal stitch to the right, and the second stitch is a diagonal stitch to the left that crosses on top of the first one.

Start by working one or more evenly spaced and separate slanted stitches in one direction. Cover each stitch with another stitch slanting in the opposite direction or work all the underneath stitches in one journey and then make a second return journey in the opposite direction, working all the top stitches. All stitches should cross in the same direction.

I love cross-stitched initials on hand towels. It is an easy project on which to begin learning this stitch.

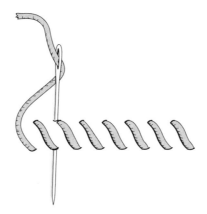

Your own designs are simple to prepare on graph paper by using different colored pencils to shade the areas that are to be cross-stitched.

Long-Armed Cross Stitch

The *long-armed* cross stitch is worked in long and short diagonal stitches whose subsequent crosses overlap. It has one "longer" stitch and one shorter stitch—unlike the basic cross stitch in which each stitch is the same length.

Bring your needle through the fabric at the stitching baseline and make a long cross stitch (diagonal) at the desired height of your stitches. Bring the needle to the back of the fabric. Now you are ready to do the "short" arm. If you are doing freehand embroidery, measure, or simply eyeball, the horizontal distance from the beginning point of the stitch to the ending point. Bring out the needle at one half of this distance to the left and on top of the stitching line.

Note that if you are working on an evenweave fabric, simply count the number of fabric threads over which you have worked the long cross stitch, divide by two, and bring up the needle at that halfway point to begin the short stitch.

Make a second diagonal cross stitch back to the baseline, and insert the needle directly below the point where needle was inserted on the top line. Bring the needle out directly below the point where it emerged on top of the line.

The long-armed stitch looks attractive on borders and makes a braided geometric pattern.

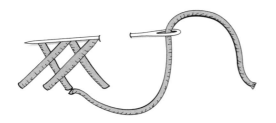

Use the long-armed cross stitch for fillings and borders.

Herringbone Stitch

The *herringbone* stitch is used for edgings and fillings, but it is also the foundation for many other stitches.

Bring your needle through your fabric on the baseline and insert it on the top line a little to the right. Next bring up the needle to the left of the top line and insert it on the baseline so that it crosses the top of the first stitch. This completes the first herringbone stitch.

The herringbone stitch is worked from left to right.

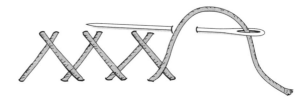

As you work the herringbone stitch, be sure to rest the thread above the needle and keep your stitches spaced evenly. Repeat the herringbone pattern as shown, spacing evenly so that the diagonals are parallel. Herringbone stitches make overlapping V patterns on the face of the fabric and parallel running stitches on the back of the fabric.

A Stitch in Time

The herringbone stitch is also known as the Russian stitch for its age-old use in that country.

Basket Stitch

Like the long-armed cross stitch, the *basket* stitch is worked from left to right. Make the first stitch by working a diagonal with your thread from the baseline to the top line, with the needle inserted vertically down through the design lines. Make the second stitch by taking a vertical stitch down toward the left and into the same holes as the two previous stitches.

The basket stitch is useful for fillings and edgings and produces a braided effect.

Zigzag Stitch

The *zigzag* stitch is created—you guessed it—by making a zigzag pattern. This is done by alternating vertical stitches and diagonal long stitches to form a row.

Create a row of alternating diagonal and vertical stitches, working from left to right. On the return row, working right to left, take vertical stitches into the same holes as the previous vertical stitches and reverse the direction of the diagonal stitches so that they cross each other.

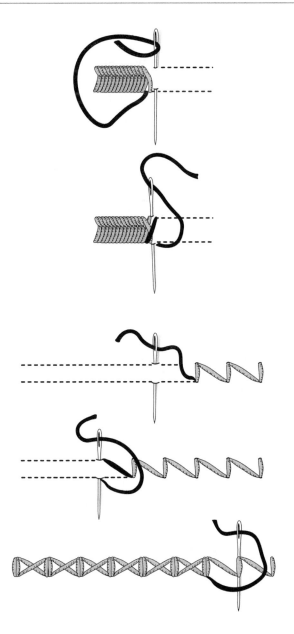

The basket stitch is similar to the long-armed stitch because it is worked with a forward and backward stitch.

With consistent stitches and practice, the zigzag stitch forms an even geometric stitch for edging linens.

The zigzag stitch is used for edgings and fillings and for geometric lattice backgrounds.

Leaf Stitch

The *leaf* stitch is a light, open stitch that is ideal for filling in leaves. This stitch looks good when it is used in combination with an outline stitch that completes the leaf shape. It is also used for borders. The size of the stitch can be varied if need be.

Bring your needle up at left of center and insert it at the right of the leaf border. Now bring up your needle a little to right of center, as shown in the following figure. Insert your needle at the left of the leaf border, and bring it up at left of center below the stitch just formed. The leaf stitch is worked upward from side to side.

The leaf stitch is ideal for filling in leaves, as its name implies.

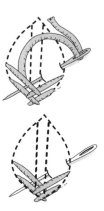

Looped Stitches

All *looped stitches* consist of loops that are held in place with small stitches. When used for outlining and for filling patterns, looped stitches create beautiful and interesting effects. Looped stitches are also used in blackwork and crewelwork. Both of these types of embroidery are discussed in more detail in Chapter 7, "Combining Stitches and Special Effects."

Clever Crafter

The chain stitch is frequently seen in Chinese and Indian embroideries. It truly is one of the most effective of all of the embroidery stitches.

Chain Stitch

The *chain* stitch is the most important of all the looped stitches. It is a versatile stitch that can be worked with fine threads or thick yarns.

Bring your needle from the back of your fabric through to the front. Loop the thread and hold it down with your left thumb. Re-insert the needle where you first brought the needle through, and bring the needle tip out a short distance below this point. Keep the thread under the tip of the needle and pull the needle through. Make the next stitch by inserting the needle into the hole from which it has just emerged.

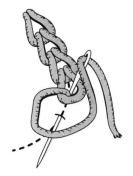

The chain stitch is the basic stitch of the looped stitches.

Lazy Daisy

The *lazy daisy* stitch is also referred to as the detached chain stitch. It is commonly used to make leaf and flower shapes as well as for filling areas. It is worked similarly to the chain stitch except that each loop is fastened down with a small tiedown stitch.

Bring your needle out at the arrow indicated in the following figure, and re-insert in the same hole, keeping the needle on top of the thread loop. Bring up the needle inside the loop, again keeping the needle on top of the thread. Finally, create the tiedown by bringing the needle over the loop and inserting it under the loop.

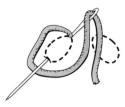

The lazy daisy stitch is similar to the chain stitch except that each loop is tacked down.

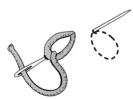

Blanket Stitch

The *blanket* stitch is universally known and sometimes referred to as the buttonhole stitch. It is perfect for edging hems and buttonholes. It is an important stitch for couching, laidwork, and cutwork (also see Chapter 7).

51

The blanket stitch is perfect for edging blankets or linens.

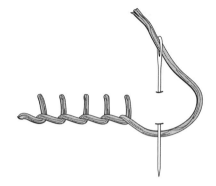

The blanket stitch is worked from left to right, bringing your thread out at the point for the looped edging. Insert the needle above and a little to the left of this point. Take a straight downward stitch, making sure that the thread is under the tip of the needle. Pull up on the stitch to make a square loop and continue the same steps to form a continuous chain.

Checkered Chain Stitch

The *checkered chain* stitch is a fancier variation of the chain stitch. It is worked with two threads of contrasting colors. Work the stitch the same as the chain stitch, but keep the color of thread that is not in use above the point of the needle.

The checkered chain stitch is a fancier variation of the chain stitch.

Open Chain

The *open chain,* or ladder, stitch forms a pattern similar to that of a ladder. It is used for bandings and for filling motifs of graduating size with varying stitch widths.

Bring your needle through the fabric at the left guideline and then insert it at the right guideline. Bring the thread out again at the left guideline with the thread under the needle. A "ladder" pattern will appear.

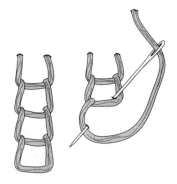

The open chain stitch forms a pattern similar to a ladder.

Feather Stitch

The *feather* stitch is similar to the blanket stitch, but the "arms" are angled. It is used for smocking (see Chapter 7), edgings, and borders. Bring your thread and needle from top to bottom. Bring your needle out at "A," and hold the thread to the left. Insert the needle at "B," and bring it out at "C," taking care to keep the loop under the needle.

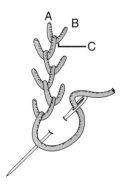

The feather stitch is similar to the blanket stitch.

Cretan Stitch

The *Cretan* stitch is a very decorative filling stitch also known as the long-armed feather. It can be worked to fit broad or narrow shapes simply by varying the stitch sizes.

Begin by bringing your needle through the middle at the left side of the guideline, with the needle pointing inward on the pattern and the thread under the tip of the needle.

Clever Crafter

The Cretan stitch takes its name from the island of Crete, where it has been used on clothing for hundreds of years.

53

Take a small stitch on the upper guideline, with the needle pointing inward toward the pattern and the thread under the needle. Repeat these steps until the shape is filled.

The Cretan stitch is a decorative filling stitch.

Knotted Stitches

Knotted stitches provide exciting textures for embroidered goods. They are formed by looping thread around a needle and then pulling the needle through the loops to form a knot or twist on the surface of the fabric.

French Knot

The *French knot* is commonly used to give a "sprinkling" effect, to denote dots, or to make a solid filling for motifs. French knots are very effective when massed together for abstract designs or landscapes. They also make a charming coat for a little sheep.

A Stitch in Time

Practice a few knotted stitches on a scrap of fabric before starting on your embroidery. It takes practice to get the tension of the knots even.

The French knot adds a dotted relief effect.

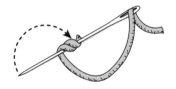

Bring your needle out at the point where you want the knot to be. Twist the needle two or three times around the thread. Turn the needle and insert it just above the point where the thread first emerged. Keeping the needle vertical, hold the working thread taut and pull the thread through to the back of the work with your left hand. For larger knots, use two or more strands of thread rather than more twists.

Coral Stitch

The *coral* stitch is a principal knotted stitch. It can be used for irregular lines, outlines, and borders, and for some fillings.

Begin working from left to right. Bring your thread out, and hold it with your left thumb along the line to be worked. Take a small stitch under and over the working thread. A loop forms below the line. Pull the thread through the loop to form the knot. The knots can be spaced at various intervals.

A Stitch in Time

Use a frame when making French knots so that both hands are free to secure the knot.

The Coral stitch is an important knotted stitch.

Bullion Stitch

The *bullion* stitch is a large, long knot that is used like the French knot but gives great impact. A cluster of bullions makes a rosette. Bullions are particularly decorative when used with different color threads, and many Chinese types of embroidery employ this method.

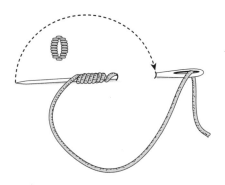

The bullion stitch adds great impact to your embroidery.

Make a backstitch that is the length you want the finished bullion knot to be. Then bring the needle halfway up at the point where it first emerged. Twist the thread

Clever Crafter

When making a knotted stitch, prevent the thread from tangling by holding down the loop of thread with your left thumb when you pull the needle through.

around the needle as many times as needed to accommodate the size of the backstitch. Hold your left thumb on the coiled thread and pull the needle through the wraps. If the wraps look uneven, gently stroke them with your needle. Now, turn the needle back to where it was inserted and pull the thread through to the back of the fabric so that the bullion knot lies flat.

Scroll Stitch

The *scroll* stitch makes a beautiful flowing line that resembles little waves of water. It is also used for borders and banding.

The Scroll stitch makes beautiful flowing lines.

Work the scroll stitch from left to right, bringing the needle out on your guideline. Loop the thread to the right and over the working thread, as shown in the figure. Pull through to form a knot. Be sure that you don't pull the thread too tightly.

Zigzag Stitch

The *zigzag* stitch is used for decorative bands and wide borders. It is worked exactly like the coral stitch but from top to bottom and in zigzag fashion as shown.

The zigzag stitch is used for decorative bands and borders.

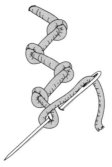

Four-Legged Knot

The *four-legged* stitch looks like an upright cross with a knot in the center. It can be used for fillings or borders when used in a row.

Begin by taking a vertical stitch and bringing the needle out at the point where the center of the knot will be.

Lay the thread across the vertical stitch to form the first step of the knot. Pass the needle under the vertical stitch and then over the working thread. Pull through to create the knot. Now take the needle to the back; the last leg of the cross is made.

The four-legged knot re-sembles an upright cross with a knot in the middle.

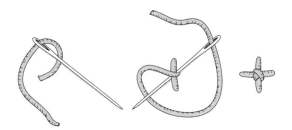

Knotted Chain Stitch

The *knotted chain* stitch, also known as the link stitch, produces a very distinctive line and looks even more striking when a thick thread is used.

Take an upward diagonal stitch, and bring out the needle just below the point where it was inserted. Pass the needle between the stitch and the fabric, keeping the looped thread to the left. Now, loop the working thread under the tip of the needle and pull through to form the knot, ready to make the next stitch.

The knotted chain stitch works well with a thick thread.

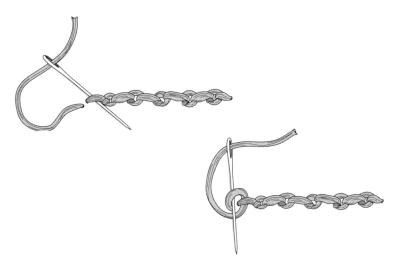

The Least You Need to Know

➤ Embroidery stitches break down into four groups: flat, crossed, looped, and knotted.

➤ Flat stitches are the easiest stitches to work.

➤ Cross stitch is one of the oldest and most popular embroidery techniques. It is easily mastered.

➤ Of all of the looped stitches, the chain stitch is the most effective stitch, especially with color and texture changes.

➤ Knotted stitches produce exciting raised textures.

Initially Speaking: The Art of Monogramming

Needlework has a long tradition as a skill for creating "useful" things, such as pillows, coasters, hand towels, and those beloved tea cozies and toaster covers. This association with utilitarian, or even frivolous, items has caused many people to consider it as more of a craft than an art form. But needleworking *is* an art, and this means you are now an artist, even if you've never considered yourself one. As an artist, learn to "sign" your work, as all great artists do. Personalizing your creations with your initials or your own signature design will be a satisfying way to complete your work. And you'll leave your mark for generations to come!

Making It Your Own

As well as "signing" your work, you can use embroidered monograms, initials, and messages to add a personal touch to gifts, home accessories, and clothing. From a single letter stitched on a dishtowel to your favorite motto on a sampler, hand-embroidered lettering is a priceless form of needlework that can help create the most

Clever Crafter

Did you know that household linens of the aristocracy were originally embroidered with motifs of crowns and coronets to signify the rank of the owner? By the eighteenth century, however, these motifs had become traditional designs used to fill in awkward spaces.

A Stitch in Time

When stitching letters, try to use a frame. This will keep the stitches even and prevent the fabric from puckering.

coveted possessions. Learning the techniques of padded satin stitch, braidwork, and openwork will add variety to your letters, as well as apply your knowledge of the stitches you have learned in previous chapters.

Whether you decide to initial your artwork or monogram a pillowcase, personalizing your needlework is a great way to become a real "artist"!

The A to Z of Monograms

Early embroidered letters were used as a practical form of identification of household linens. The markings were usually somewhat hidden, placed on the upper right corner of pillowcases, towels, and sheets. Today monogrammed items are fashionable with the lettering front and center, in all sizes and in matching or contrasting thread.

Embroidered letters were also often used to stitch messages that revealed religious beliefs or had moral overtones. In the eighteenth and nineteenth centuries, young girls learned messages of morality along with the art of embroidery. Embroidered valentines and postcards were seen in the nineteenth century, as well as hearthside inscriptions such as "Home Sweet Home."

Know Your Alphabets

The following charts provide a cross-stitch alphabet, an alphabet for satin stitch, and a numerals list. You can work the cross-stitch alphabet directly from the chart, because each square equals one stitch. The satin stitch alphabet and the numerals chart need to be traced and transferred to your fabric. See Chapter 4, "Technique Chic," to read up on transferring techniques.

By stitching and practicing your numerals, you can date all of your embroideries with ease!

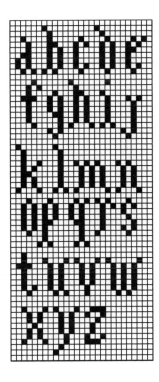

Don't be afraid of curvy letters. Practice a few on a scrap piece of fabric, and you will feel very confident about stitching curvy letters such as "s" and "c."

The satin stitch gives letters a polished look.

Stitching Simple Letters and Monograms

For effective letter embroidery, the letters must be stitched with even stitches and defined lines in order for them to be clearly readable. The next three figures show you letters worked in three different techniques and stitches: chain, cross, and satin stitch.

These stitches offer the quickest way to work letters that have already been marked on fabric. You can embellish the letters with other techniques (discussed further on in this chapter) or with a simple frame of stitching. For a classic look, leave the letters or monogram unadorned.

> **A Stitch in Time**
>
> You can trace letters from books and magazines! Transfer the outlines onto your fabric by using the transfer methods from Chapter 4.

An easy stitch for free-form letters, the chain stitch can be effectively outlined with the stem stitch.

Cross-stitched letters are easily spaced by using the weave of the fabric as a grid pattern.

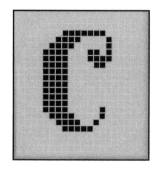

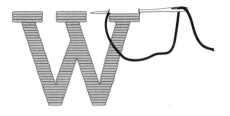

The satin stitch must be worked with even and smooth stitches. Practice one letter before embarking on an entire monogram.

Padding Your Lettering

Padding is a technique used to give emphasis, definition, and dimensionality to a motif. The padding slightly raises the stitching above the surface of the fabric. An easy way to pad a motif is to work running stitches within and around the motif, following its shape. I often suggest that you use the same color for the padding as you do for the satin stitch that you stitch over the padding.

Oftentimes, padded stitched lettering is worked in the same color as the background fabric. For example, a white-on-white look could be a white linen sheet having a raised, or "padded," monogram in a white satin stitch. The effect of such a monochromatic combination is truly handsome!

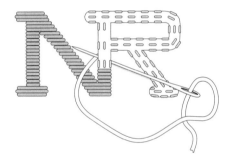

Work the outline of the letter in running stitches, and fill in with satin stitch. See Chapter 5 for a refresher on the satin stitch.

Clever Crafter

Use the unique "negative" satin stitch for a clever visual effect on monograms and crests. It is the reverse of the padded satin stitch because you stitch in the negative areas around the letters and not the letters themselves. To begin, outline the background of the monogram and around the letter. Use the padded satin stitch to fill in the background. Your letters will become visible as you fill in the background.

Braid and Ribbon Lettering

Fine braiding or ribbon can make very effective lettering. The ribbon or braid is attached, or tied down, with small, closely spaced stitches using a technique called *couching* (see Chapter 7, "Combining Stitches and Special Effects," for more). Press the short ends of the braid or ribbon to the wrong side of your fabric, and tack in place with two or three small straight stitches. On narrow ribbon or braid, stitch down the middle, and on wider ribbon stitch both edges to make the piece lie flat.

A Stitch in Time

When using braid or ribbon for lettering, try to use one continuous piece so that there are no breaks in the line of braid or ribbon.

Patterned ribbon adds another visual dimension to the lettering.

Using Openwork

Openwork provides an interesting background for lettering, especially a satin-stitched letter. In this technique, stitches form an "open" pattern that creates a setting for the letter.

The openwork wave stitch is an example of how this technique can be used to fill in a background area. The wave pattern consists of a series of rows of vertical, evenly spaced stitches that are worked across the background of the letter area. Always embroider the letter first and then the background. It is easier to stitch the openwork around the letter as opposed to doing the letter over the background of openwork. The openwork forms an attractive lattice-like effect that is easily accomplished by following the directions given next. Border the letter with a stem stitch to emphasize the letter and separate it from the background. (See Chapter 5, "In Stitches," for more on the stem stitch.)

The background of open-work stitches nicely shows off the satin-stitched letter.

To begin, work a row of small, evenly spaced vertical stitches. Bring your needle out below and to the right of the last stitch and, working backward, make a row of "V-like" loops by passing your needle under the vertical stitches.

Continue to make the same V loops on the following rows by passing the needle under the pairs of stitch bases in the row above.

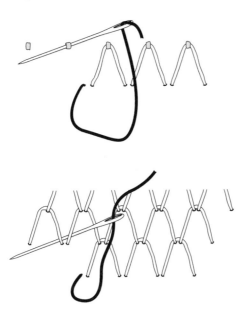

Openwork wave stitch: Steps 1 and 2.

Clever Crafter

You can embellish your letters or monograms with stitched flowers, leaves, or other motifs pertinent to the letters. For example, if you embroider the word "violet" on your fabric, you may want to stitch purple flowers that resemble violets around the letters.

Needlework 101

Sampler comes from the Latin word *exemplum,* meaning "an example to be followed."

Clever Crafter

Are you visiting a museum soon? Check out the decorative arts section. Many museums have fabulous collections of embroidered samplers (sometimes you have to ask to see them). A notable collection is found at the Shelburne Museum in Shelburne, Vermont.

The Simplicity of Samplers

Today, *samplers* are typically very personalized items, used for display and gifts. Originally, however, samplers were used as a reference tool, a way to record—on fabric—the many different stitches that the needleworker might need with many left, unsigned. They stitched openwork patterns and worked in parallel bands on narrow strips of linen, for embroidery on household linens. In the sixteenth century, the first stitch book was published, and this paved the way for the use of samplers for more decorative purposes.

The sixteenth and early seventeenth centuries are characterized by spot samplers (motifs done randomly), and the later seventeenth century by band samplers, bands of patterns worked on a long, narrow cloth. In fact, the seventeenth century is known as the Golden Age of samplers because of the complicated techniques, sophisticated design, and luxury materials (pearls, jewels, silk, gold) used in these samplers. The early eighteenth century is associated with pictorial samplers, including pious verses and alphabets surrounded by a decorative border (what you date as seventeenth century).

By the late eighteenth and nineteenth centuries, the sampler had become a technical exercise by which young girls learned moral values and the alphabet and numbers. Other types of schoolroom samplers taught geography—map samplers (not very accurate), arithmetic—multiplication tables samplers, and domestic skills—plain sewing and darning samplers. Although childhood samplers marked the decline of the sampler, their very unsophisticated nature and the childish mistakes make them the most charming and popular of antique samplers to collect. What we think of today as a typical sampler is actually the square pictorial style.

To create your own sampler, follow the example in Chapter 10, "An Easy Embroidery Project from Start to Finish." You can also buy inexpensive kits that have a variety of sampler designs. Re-create museum samplers by studying them. Or design your own and stitch a message that reveals your family's philosophy. Add the alphabet at the bottom, along with a line of numbers and maybe a stitched picture of your home at the top, with people on either side—you and your important others. Be sure to stitch your name and the date along with the place you live (city and state).

Although today we often see letters on samplers spaced evenly, I like to see quirky stitching where you may have run out of room and squeezed some letters together. This imperfect look, emulating the childish efforts of young stitchers two hundred years ago, adds tremendous character and panache.

Clever Crafter

Some of the most cherished samplers are those that commemorate weddings. It is usually the bride's most treasured gift!

The Least You Need to Know

➤ The alphabet can be worked in various embroidery stitches and used as part of a design or for the practice of needlework.

➤ Monograms add a personal touch to household linens, clothing, and gifts, as well as providing identification for your work.

➤ Chain, padded satin, cross stitch, and couching are different stitches and techniques for embroidering letters or monograms.

➤ Samplers historically were used as fabric notebooks to record, in thread, examples of various embroidery stitches and motifs. Today they depict familiar, favored motifs of home, family, animals, and personal messages with the embroiderer's initials and date of completion.

Part 3
Advanced Embroidery

There are tons and tons of wonderful stitches for embroidery! You might have even seen books that are dedicated entirely to embroidery stitches. Although I couldn't fit every stitch in this book, I have included a mix of easy, popular, and tricky stitches for you to learn.

I've also included some interesting techniques that will make your projects the envy of all your friends. When you've practiced a few advanced stitches, try your hand at the easy project in Chapter 10. Think you're ready for the next level? Want to kick your embroidery up a notch? Welcome to Advanced Embroidery!

Combining Stitches and Special Effects

Now that you have mastered the beginner basics, you are ready for the next level. This is the stage where embroidery becomes a little easier and more fun because you can now start experimenting with what you know. Learning more interesting stitches and how to combine stitches to create special effects will help advance your skill to master the craft!

Special Techniques

Couching, laidwork, and smocking are special techniques that will broaden your embroidery knowledge. Couching is a method of securing threads that have been laid on the fabric surface. Laidwork forms gridlike patterns, and smocking eliminates fullness and provides a decorative pattern.

Couching

Couching, is an embroidery technique used to attach "laid threads" (threads that have been placed to lie flat on the fabric). The laid threads are secured with a separate strand of thread and small stitches taken at intervals. This method is often used to

work fragile metal or gold threads. Such threads can be easily damaged if passed through fabric and so are nicely worked by laying them on the surface of the fabric. More than one thread can be laid together to create bold lines or outlines. Couching is also a good method to use for filling large areas of solid color.

Working from left to right, position the thread or threads on your fabric, using your thumb to hold them in place. Bring out the working couching thread from underneath the fabric, just below the laid thread. Secure the laid thread at regular intervals with a couching stitch, as shown in the following figure. Finish at the end of the line by taking both the couching thread and the laid thread to the back of the fabric.

A Stitch in Time

Couching was developed to show off threads that are either too valuable, too brittle, or too delicate to be pulled through fabric.

Generally the laid threads are heavier than the couching thread, which is typically a finer weight.

If you want to continue couching, turn the loose laid thread to the right and stitch across the turn. Turn work upside down, and couch the second row of threads next to the first, placing stitches in between the stitches of the previous row.

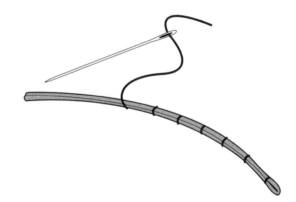

Laidwork

Laidwork is a version of couching and is usually used for covering large areas. It is a quick and very effective way of filling both backgrounds and motifs because you use long stitches in a grid fashion. These stitches are secured at the intersecting threads with a separate thread. Laidwork can be very decorative, forming a pattern of simple stripes, chevrons, swirls, or trellises. The easiest laidwork pattern produces a grid effect, as shown in the next figure.

1. Work horizontal stitches, evenly spaced, across the area to be filled.

2. Create the grid effect by laying vertical stitches across the horizontal threads in the same way.

3. Bring the couching thread from the back of the fabric through to the front at the top left corner of the grid and stitch the intersection of the vertical and horizontal threads with a small slanted stitch.

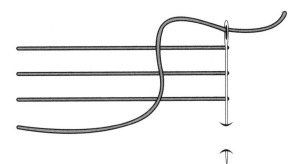

Steps 1, 2, and 3 for laidwork.

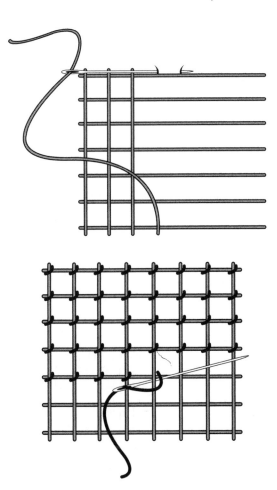

Smocking

Smocking reduces fullness in fabric with a very attractive gathered stitch pattern. It is a popular method used for shaping and decorating adult and young children's clothing. Baby items decorated in smocking become precious heirlooms.

Any type of fabric can be smocked as long as it is supple enough to be gathered. Checked or dot patterned fabrics are popular because the checks or dots can be used as a guideline for gathering stitches.

Smocking is worked by gathering fabric into even-sized folds, called pleats, before the garment or piece is assembled. Make sure you start with fabric that is about three times the actual finished width of the garment or item so that you have enough fabric for the pleats.

Printed transfer papers are available in needlework shops or craft stores. These are transfer papers marked with equally-spaced smocking-dots that can be ironed on the face of the fabric to give you a guide for stitching. Another option is to check with quilt stores, fabric shops, and stitchery shops, because they sometimes offer pleating services.

When preparing your fabric for smocking, gather the back of the fabric in rows, picking up a small piece of fabric at each dot. There are several stitches to use for this technique (see the following sections), depending on the design you are trying to achieve. After you have worked all of your rows, tie the thread ends together in pairs.

If you are smocking a solid fabric, you will need to mark some dots to use as a guide for gathering.

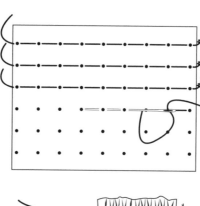

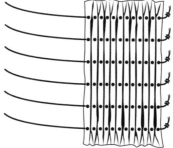

Smocking Stitches

A wide variety of smocking patterns can be formed from any of the basic stitches. For the purposes of this book, I've chosen stitches that are worked on the right side of the fabric, from left to right, so as not to confuse you. In England, some smocking is done from the back side of the fabric.

Start in the upper right corner for your first stitch. Be sure to hold the needle parallel to the gathering threads, and take the stitches at about one third of the depth of each pleat. A good trick is to leave the first gathered row free of stitches so that you can join one smocked panel to another. Simple attractive patterns can be achieved with one stitch, or intricate ones with a combination of stitches. Remember to keep the gaps between rows small and tight to prevent the pleats from puffing out.

Stem Stitch

With your gathered fabric, work a basic *stem* stitch (explained in Chapter 5, "In Stitches") as the top row of smocking. To do this, bring the needle out to the left of the first pleat. Next, take a stitch through the top of each fold, keeping the thread below the needle as you work.

Needlework 101

The word **smocking** comes from the old English word *smock*, meaning a "shift" or "chemise"—an article of clothing that is worn as a top.

Decorator's Do's and Don'ts

When using transfer papers, *do* make sure that each dot falls on the weave line of the fabric; if not, the fabric is likely to stretch and wrinkle.

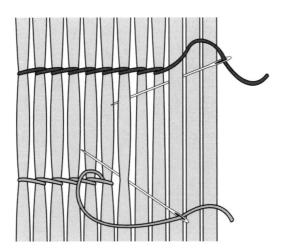

The stem stitch creates accordion-style pleats.

Cable Stitch

The *cable* stitch in smocking is worked with stem stitches that form a cable (your thread) that goes in and out of the folds of the fabric.

To start, bring the needle to the surface of your fabric through the first fold on the left. Insert the needle horizontally and work stem stitches into each fold with the thread alternately above and then below the needle.

The smocking cable stitch creates more decorative folds than a plain smocking stem stitch.

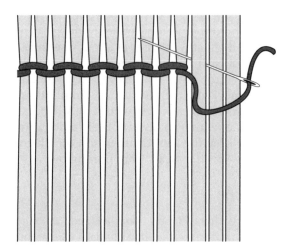

Honeycomb Stitch

The *honeycomb* stitch is aptly named due to its honeycomb appearance. The honeycomb stitch is worked along two lines of gathering stitches.

Working from left to right, bring the needle out on the first line and make a backstitch to draw together the second and first folds. Now, take a second stitch over the two folds, bringing the needle out at the lower line of gathering stitches and between the first and second fold. Make another backstitch to draw the third and second folds together. Return the needle to the first line again, only this time at the third fold. Draw the fourth and third folds together. Continue working in the same way, alternately up and down to the end of each row.

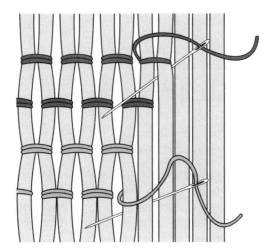

Honeycomb stitches form a smocking pattern that looks like the inside of a beehive.

Beadwork

Beadwork is a form of embroidery that uses beads and sequins applied with a needle and thread and special techniques. Beads and sequins have been used throughout the ages to add richness and sparkle to textiles and clothing. They are the most effective way of transforming simple patterns into beautiful and exotic designs.

Beads and sequins have many fun applications. They can be used to create an entire picture, trim the hem of a skirt, highlight wall hangings and pillows, and add the finishing touch on a small project (such as two single beads for the eyes of an elephant).

Clever Crafter

The difference between today's beadwork and beadwork from the past lies in the beads themselves: The sparkle and glitter on old beads came from real jewels and gold and silver spangles. Today's beads are made of tin, plastic, and glass.

Stitching with Beads

On the spot where you plan to place your bead, bring your needle out from the back of the fabric to the front and thread the bead. Use an ordinary sewing needle for beads with large holes, but a special beading needle (obtainable at bead shops, craft stores, and stitching shops) for beads with small holes.

Use strong thread for items that will receive handling or use. Special beading thread and beading wire are available. Another idea is to make your own beading thread by waxing your thread with beeswax to strengthen it. Or you can stitch through each bead twice to add strength.

The sequins are built up on one another, thus hiding the stitches.

If the bead is round, insert the needle back through the same hole in the fabric. If the bead is a long cylindrical one (like a bugle bead), hold down the bead with your thumb and insert the needle close to the edge of the bead; pull the thread through to the back of the fabric. Repeat these steps to form a row of beads.

Applying Sequins

Sequins can be applied to fabric with invisible or visible stitching. You can decide whether you want the thread to be decorative for a contrasting effect, or hidden so that only the sequins show. Use sequins to border collars or cuffs, or scatter them on an embroidery to add sparkle.

To create invisible stitches, overlap the sequins and work a backstitch into the left side of the first set. To do this, place a single sequin on the fabric and take the needle through its eye (hole). Place another sequin on top of the first sequin—half covering it. Make sure the right edge covers the eye of the one before. Bring your needle back up at the left edge of the second sequin and into the eye, at the same time inserting the needle into the eye of the previous sequin.

To stitch on only one side of a sequin, bring the needle from the back of your fabric through to the front and then insert it through the eye of the sequin. Make a backstitch over the right side of the sequin. Bring your needle out to the left, ready to thread through the eye of a second sequin. Place the second sequin next to the previous one, edge to edge. Secure the rest of your sequins this way.

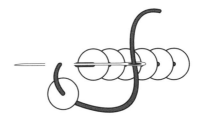

The thread becomes a decorative feature when stitches are worked on one side only.

Combining Stitches for Special Effects

Once you've mastered some of the basic embroidery stitches from Chapter 5, try combining stitches to produce some unique effects with the most time-honored forms of embroidery. Some that we will discuss are crewelwork, stumpwork, whitework, and blackwork.

Crewelwork

Crewelwork is a traditional form of embroidery that combines outline stitches for borders and broad stitches for filling in shapes. These two types of stitches are used to form free-flowing motifs like trees and flowers. Traditional motifs have always been animals, birds, and naturalistic scenes. The basic shapes are stitched in an outline stitch and then filled in with broad stitches, such as the satin stitch, or textural ones, such as French knots.

Stumpwork

Stumpwork is a technique dating from the seventeenth century that makes embroidery three-dimensional. It is a combination of padded appliqué (cutout shapes that are sewn on a fabric and stuffed with batting) and embroidery stitches such as the padded satin stitch, couching, and the various knotted stitches. In the elaborate stumpwork creations of the seventeenth century, fine wire was incorporated to provide shape and support, for example, to make a butterfly's wing raise up for flight.

Needlework 101

Crewelwork derives its name from the crewel wool with which it is worked (the word *crewel* comes from the Anglo-Saxon word "cleowen," meaning ball of thread).

To try some simple stumpwork, cut out a shape, just a bit larger than the finished size, and baste it to the fabric. If you use felt, it won't fray, making it a perfect choice. Leave a small section open, and stuff some batting into it to pad the shape. Sew the opening shut, and decorate the shape by bordering it with such stitches as the padded satin stitch, couching, or knotted stitches. Remove the basting stitches.

Stumpwork adds a three-dimensional quality to your needlework.

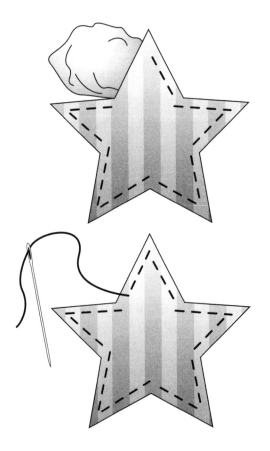

Whitework

Whitework is the name given to any white embroidery used on a white ground. It is often seen on bed linens, blouses, handkerchiefs, and table linens.

You can create monochromatic contrasts by mixing a rough, no-sheen fabric, such as linen, with a shiny thread, such as high-sheen pearl cotton.

Blackwork

Blackwork is a very old form of embroidery that is traditionally worked with dark thread on a lighter, linen fabric, the usual combination being black thread on white fabric. Blackwork is based on a counted-thread technique, with patterns being stitched in backstitch, running stitch, and cross stitch. Outline stitches, such as the chain stitch, stem stitch, and couching, are used to add a finishing touch to the patterns.

A Stitch in Time

Add even more contrast to whitework by using the cutwork method, a type of embroidery in which the ground fabric is cut away. Trace some small circles or other shapes onto your fabric. With pearl cotton thread, work a double outline around the shape, using a small running stitch. Then work a blanket (buttonhole) stitch (see Chapter 5), just wide enough to cover the running stitch. Now, with small, sharp scissors, carefully cut away the interior fabric, revealing a hole shaped like your drawing. This leaves a very attractive lacy pattern.

Blackwork is traditionally worked with black thread on white linen.

Now that you have some ideas for experimenting, it's time to try some out. When you start creating your own combinations of stitches and techniques, there's no turning back—you'll probably never buy a kit again!

81

The Least You Need to Know

➤ Couching is an effective way to secure threads that cannot be drawn through the fabric. Laidwork is usually used to decoratively fill and cover large areas of your embroidery.

➤ Smocking is a way of reducing fullness in a fabric as well as decorating it.

➤ Beadwork is a very old embroidery method that adds sparkle and richness to a fabric.

➤ Combining different stitches results in very special effects, such as crewelwork, stumpwork, whitework, and blackwork.

Chapter 8

Designing Your Own Embroidery

In This Chapter

➤ Preparing your own free-form designs by studying others

➤ Learning some design tips

➤ Picking up special techniques for pictorial embroidery

With your new knowledge of stitches and techniques, you are ready to explore some ideas for designing your own embroideries. Designing and crafting your own needlework is one of most fulfilling aspects of needlework. You can be proud to be the creator and the maker of a handmade item!

The Forming of Forms

What is an embroidery design? A simple, single leaf stitched on a pillowcase? A monogram on a hand towel? A lilac on a dinner napkin? All of these are considered embroideries. But wait, add smaller motifs to create an edging for the monogrammed hand towel and *now* you have a design.

With the techniques that you learned in Chapter 4, "Technique Chic," you can actually enlarge a tiny, single motif and use it as the central pattern on a larger piece, such as a pillow or bath towel. If you repeat the single motif at regular intervals, the ground fabric will be covered with a pretty, overall pattern and the motif will become the entire design. Bands of different colors and stitches can be used to make a design, and you can even alternate stripes of stitches with plain ground fabric. The sky is the limit with embroidery designs!

If you are just beginning to learn embroidery, go easy. For an original design, start with an easy pattern having a couple of stitches for the motif and maybe a third stitch for a special textured effect. Practice stitching part of your idea on a scrap piece of fabric before attempting the real thing. For more-detailed designs, sketch them on a piece of paper or on your fabric so that you have a visual picture to follow. Experiment with different methods; soon you'll find the best fit for you.

Decorator's Do's and Don'ts

Choose a subject that you love! You will have an incentive to complete your project. If you love dogs, then stitch an image of your pet. Don't stitch cats if they are of no interest—you'll never finish it.

Inspiration for Designs

Where can you find inspiration for your embroidery designs? Look out the window and take in what nature has to offer. A flower? A tree? An entire landscape? Go to a museum and review some paintings or photographs that appeal to you. The decorative arts section usually has antique textiles with embroidery that you could imitate or adapt as an embellishment. Not only will you find ideas for texture and design in these old embroideries, but you will also see classic combinations of colors, patterns, threads, stitches, and background fabric. Porcelain patterns are another source that can be copied and embroidered. Book illustrations and wallpapers may inspire you as well.

Every original embroidery design begins with an idea. An idea is sparked by your daily life and outside influences. Maybe you saw a piece of trim on your neighbor's drapery? What about the dress pattern you liked that was worn by the woman in a painting? Go through your closets. Look at the edgings on your clothes. The possibilities are endless!

Cultivate Your Ideas

Cultivate your ideas through exposure to every piece of needlework you can get your hands on! Gain confidence in some of your ideas by comparing them to those found in catalogs, needlework magazines, and museum pieces. Home decor magazines often show unusual uses of needlework as well as interiors that have been accessorized with needlework accent pillows and linens.

Clever Crafter

In ancient China, embroidery symbolized rank or circumstance. Wishes for the wearer were also stitched on clothing. Flowers and fruits were significant images on marriage garments. The lotus symbolized fruitfulness and purity, while the pomegranate represented hopes of fertility.

Study different styles of embroidery by attending needlework exhibits and art fairs or by investigating your local library's collection of embroidery books. Try secondhand bookshops for inexpensively priced embroidery books. Record the embroidery techniques or designs you like or would like to imitate. Jot down the color combinations. Be on the lookout for unexpected inspiration: perhaps an embroidered cocktail bag on the arm of a woman at the opera, a pattern on a silk scarf worn by a woman on the bus, or a beautiful bouquet of flowers at the doctor's office. Your Aunt Ethel may have a fabulous wall covering whose motifs and colors would make a smashing embroidery piece.

Subscribe to a monthly needlework magazine and see what other needleworkers are doing. Refer to Appendix A, "Resources for Novice Needleworkers," to help in your quest for knowledge about embroidery.

Now File Those Ideas

Start a filing system for those new ideas. Label file folders by categories. Pattern, color, embroidered piece, and stitches are examples of categories. Use a sturdy cardboard file box, drawer of a filing cabinet, or a decorative wicker filing basket to hold your files. Read, peruse, cut, and file. These folders will form the master resource for your ideas on many projects. If you can sketch, keep a pad of paper and colored pencils handy so that you can capture a design that you can't physically take with you. You can't draw? Carry a disposable camera; it's handy, easy to carry around, and better than your memory!

Filing your ideas will gradually help you focus on your vision. The accumulated pictures, brochures, photos, and sketches will become pieces of a puzzle that you are putting together to reveal a style suited to you and your tastes.

Helpful Hints for Preparing Your Design

Deciding on the size of your design, type of fabric, and method of stitching will help you on your way with an overall design scheme for your embroidery.

Design Decisions

Go through your files and select designs that suit your project. You need to decide if you can transfer them as is. These designs may not be the right size. You may need to enlarge or reduce them as you learned in Chapter 4.

Type of Fabric

The ground fabric you choose depends on the type of design, kind of stitches, and the threads you use, as discussed in Chapter 3, "Tools of the Trade." You might choose a printed fabric and then stitch the outlines of the motifs or embroider the motif itself. A solid even weave fabric would be appropriate for cross stitch embroidery. A light colored background fabric could show off dark colored threads but also display a subtle pattern with a similar color thread. Using opposite materials can be attractive, such as a rough burlap background with smooth silk thread. Use your imagination and your design will be unique.

A Stitch in Time

Did you know that outlining a pattern can cover up any "less than perfect" worked edges?

Clever Crafter

Voiding is typically found in Greek and Assisi embroideries.

Outlines

Outlines will really help to define the shape of your designs. For a subtle outline, choose a thread color similar to the color of the shape being outlined. For emphasis, choose a contrasting thread color. Metallic threads might add just the spark that your design needs. Couching the outline of a design is another way to add emphasis. (See Chapter 7, "Combining Stitches and Special Effects.")

Use several rows of outlining to add even greater accent. And don't forget—the outlining doesn't have to be straight stitching! Chain stitches add a curvaceous edge to the pattern.

Voiding

A unique way to design embroidery is to use the *voiding* method in which the motif is left unstitched and instead the background is filled in. Start by outlining the motif. Then fill in the background around the motif, leaving the actual interior of the motif "undone." You could use a stem stitch for outlining the motif and a satin stitch for filling in the background.

Like outlining, couching also enhances the outlines of motifs and can be effectively combined with the voiding method.

Backgrounds

As you learned in the previous section on voiding, the background of a pattern or motif can be either left exposed or stitched in various ways. It's common to think of your background fabric as less significant because it's in the background. True, the ground fabric is the means used to create your embroidery, but it is also a big part of your design.

There are other ways to use your background fabric that will complement your design and create special effects. Try stitching geometric shapes at different intervals so as to "dot" the background and leave the spaces between the "dots" unworked. An overall pattern is achieved. You could also try couching the outlines of your motifs for extra emphasis of the exposed background.

Color and Thread Combos

It is amazing how so many embroideries can be "engineered" by combining different options for threads and stitches. Simply by changing the colors of the threads but using the same stitch, a pattern can take on a new look. Even with the same color thread and the same stitch, you can develop a new pattern by changing the direction of the stitch.

➤ **Same stitch, different threads.** Try using the same stitch on identical designs but introducing different types of threads to achieve a textural effect. The old saying "opposites attract" is a good philosophy to use in your embroidery! Highlight shiny threads with *matte* threads, and use wool threads to highlight glossy threads.

➤ **Same stitch, same thread.** Many embroideries are worked in the same stitch throughout and the same color of thread. The pattern is formed by the arrangement of the stitches. You will read in the next section on pictorial embroidery that the same thread and stitch can be used to form pictures. Shiny threads, such as silk worked in a satin stitch vertically and horizontally, will reflect light differently, thus creating a pattern with the change in color tones. Matte threads, such as wool, have less dramatic changes but still create a pattern with different directions of stitches.

➤ **Same color, different stitches.** Different stitches used together form rich patterns, as can be seen in whitework and blackwork. A sampler done in one color throughout but with various embroidery stitches can be a beautiful way to use the "same color thread but different stitch" concept.

Decorator's Do's and Don'ts

Don't be afraid to stitch a pattern using a thread that is similar in color to the background fabric and combining them with the voiding method. A linen background with a similar color thread is a stunning use of tone on tone. This will create texture, which is a visual delight.

Needlework 101

Matte is any finish that is not shiny.

Different Color Effects

By using complementary colors, colors in the same family, you can create shading and illumination. For subtle accents, a slowly graduating effect is achieved by using several tones from dark to light. For a heathered look, thread your needle with various tones of the same color such as reds, pinks, and raspberries. Some threads come pre-dyed in several different shades and tones that create an antiqued effect when stitched. The faded look is already built in!

Pictorial Embroidery

In *pictorial embroidery,* as the name suggests, pictures are formed with stitches. Ani0imals and birds are easily depicted with threads and stitches that resemble fur and feathers. Human faces and skin are a little harder to portray, but nature—animals, water, trees, the sky—can be easily embroidered by following these hints for choosing stitches:

➤ **Fur and hair.** For straight fur or hair, use the satin stitch in various lengths. For rigid fur, use fillings of a buttonhole stitch. For wooly fur or curly hair, use French knots. For wavy fur or hair, use the chain stitch.

➤ **Feathers.** Use satin stitches of various lengths and directions to follow the line of a feather.

➤ **Sky and water.** For calming effects, use flat stitches. For storms, use swirling or circular stitch arrangements, such as the chain stitch, or couch partial circles to resemble water movement or cloud shapes.

➤ **Wind and rain.** For gusts of wind, suddenly change the direction of your stitches. For rain, use irregularly sized strokes of top stitching.

➤ **Landscapes.** To create a sense of distance, use long stitches in the background and shorter ones in foreground.

➤ **Faces.** Although faces are one of the harder items to stitch, try using the stem stitch in concentric circles. Start at the cheekbone and work outward in wider circles. Change the tones of your thread to add shading and dimension. The features can be added on top in fine detail. Split stitch and satin stitch are alternatives to try.

Clever Crafter

Ancient Chinese embroideries often portrayed water in gold couched coils.

The Least You Need to Know

➤ Cultivate inspiration through exposure to museums, home decor books, magazines, clothing patterns, and various forms of needlework.

➤ Explore different combinations of thread color and stitch type. You will be amazed at the variety you can achieve.

➤ By combining different tones of the same color thread (monochromatic), you can create illumination and shading in your work.

➤ For pictorial embroidery, nature scenes and faces can be created by working standard stitches in new ways.

Chapter 9

The Embroiderer's Finishing Touch

> ### In This Chapter
>
> ➤ Learning the art of blocking and mounting
>
> ➤ Framing it yourself or going to a pro
>
> ➤ Cleaning, caring, and storing embroideries

When your embroidery is finished, you need to decide what you will do with it. Will you frame it or make it into a pillow? Apply it to clothing or cover your piano bench? The possibilities are almost endless.

Once you have decided how you'd like to finish your embroidery, you must prepare it. First, you might need to straighten it a bit if it has become distorted during stitching. Although most pieces need only a light pressing, some embroideries need to be stretched and straightened by using a technique called "blocking." And if you plan to hang your embroidery as wall decor, you will need to mount and frame your piece. It's also good to learn about cleaning, care, and storage of old and new embroideries, since dust, dirt, and insects are the main enemies of embroidered textiles.

Necessary Tools

Finishing your embroidery requires a few tools, most of which you already have in your home. An iron and a soft towel for blocking your finished work are important, along with straight pins (the rust-proof kind used for sewing) and soft cotton fabric. For mounting, the basic tools are cardboard, thread, and needles. Framing will require some small framing nails, wire, screw eyes, cardboard, and maybe an optional mat.

You'll also need supplies to clean and treat your piece if it is washable. Some cleaning agents are as basic as a gentle cleaner and water; stains may require astringents such as rubbing alcohol or white vinegar.

Keep finishing and cleaning supplies for your work handy in a designated area or collect them in a basket. Just having your finishing tools close by will encourage you to complete your needlework. Too many beginner needleworkers become frustrated when they cannot find their tools, and they end up leaving their work unfinished. Take to heart the French saying about cooking: *"Mise en place"*—have everything in its place before starting any project!

The Finishing Touch

When you have sewn your last stitch to complete your embroidery design you still have a few steps to go before you can say you have actually "finished" your needlework. You must prepare it for its intended use by getting it into shape if there was any distortion during stitching, or preparing it for framing if you choose to hang it on a wall.

Blocking

Blocking is the process of straightening an embroidery that has become distorted during stitching and restoring it to its original shape. To do this, soak the embroidery in cold water, wrap it in a towel to remove excess moisture (don't wring it), and pin it to a board for straightening. Blocking also removes creases and gives a professional look to your piece.

Always make sure that your fabrics and threads are *colorfast* before any blocking occurs. Otherwise, the color could run and all your hard work might be ruined! Older embroideries are more prone to this. Most of today's fabrics are colorfast, but never take a chance! To test, press a wet cotton ball onto some of the threads to see if any dye is transferred to the cotton ball. If so, you will have to block your embroidery dry.

> **Needlework 101**
>
> **Colorfast** refers to dyes in fabrics or threads that will not run when wet.

Follow these steps for colorfast fabrics and threads if your embroidery needs straightening. Skip step one if embroidery is not colorfast.

1. Soak the embroidery in cold water. Roll in a clean towel to remove excess moisture.

2. Cover a soft board like a cork bulletin board with cotton or plastic. Pin your embroidery at each corner, keeping the pins on the outside of the stitching. Gently stretch the piece as you pin at one-inch intervals, starting at center. Leave pinned until dry.

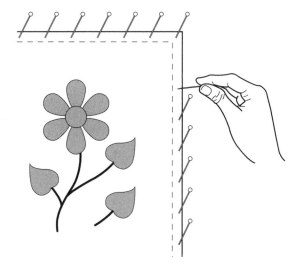

Be sure you leave the pins in place until your embroidery is completely dry.

Mounting

Mounting prepares your work for framing. You will need a piece of stiff cardboard or foamcore. The cardboard should be at least the size of the needlework, and preferably larger to allow for a margin to show beyond the design. When mounting, you will need to fold the edges of your fabric to the back of the cardboard, so be sure that the cardboard is sturdy enough for this.

Decorator's Do's and Don'ts

A scorch mark is not part of the design! Never put an iron on the right side of your embroidery work. It may scorch the piece and flatten the stitches. Instead, place your piece right side down on a padded surface. Cover it with a cloth (damp or dry, depending on the fabric). Press very gently at the proper setting for your fabric type, lifting—not sliding—your iron as you progress from area to area.

Some designs may require a very small border of fabric, whereas others may need to have a significant amount of fabric showing. For example, a small monogram may be framed in a large-scale frame so that it stands out from the background fabric. An entire landscape may meet the edges of the frame without any border of background fabric showing at all. Critique each work separately, and recall some of your newly learned design elements from Chapter 2, "Well-Designed Needle Art," to help you make decisions. To mount your embroidery, first fold the side edges of your fabric to the back side of the cardboard. Use a strong thread such as button thread to lace the edges back and forth as shown. Adjust the lacing threads so that your work is stretched smoothly across the board. When you are satisfied with the look of the piece, pull the stitches to tighten them and secure the lacing thread with a few backstitches.

Now fold back the top and bottom edges and lace in the same way. Your work is ready to be framed.

Pull the lacing threads firmly and evenly to ensure that your work is smoothly stretched and ready for framing.

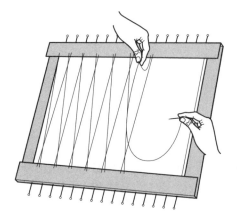

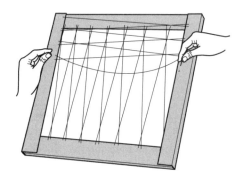

Framing

If you choose to frame your own needlework, after blocking and mounting it, you will need to find a frame that fits. You can add a mat to cover any gaps that might appear with a noncustom frame. Never trim your embroidery until you have selected the proper-size cardboard to mount and frame.

Take both your mounted piece and the measurements when you buy a frame. Hold your piece up to several different types of frames so that you can get an idea of the finished look. You may find the perfect frame, but it may come with a mat that needs to be resized to accommodate your work. No problem. Use an Exacto knife and a ruler (wait until you get home of course!) to trim the inside area of your mat board.

Selecting a frame that is ready-made or using one you already have is the most inexpensive way to frame your embroidery. However, if you are nervous about doing the framing yourself, you may want to get an estimate from a professional framer.

Decorator's Do's and Don'ts

Don't be ordinary! And don't use unattractive plastic frames that might be included in your kit. Mix traditional embroideries with contemporary frames like a piece of plain glass (that actually has no frame!) and clips that holds the glass and work together. Use a weathered wooden frame for a fancy crewelwork done in white wool on white linen.

Professional Framers

A custom framer is the easiest way to have your work framed, but also the most expensive. However, you have the advantage of being able to select from a cajillion different types and styles of frames, as well as mat colors and types. Another advantage of professional framing is that the framer will back the piece with a protective cover and attach the correct-gauge wire for hanging. A piece of glass or Plexiglas will protect the frontside as well as show off your hard work.

Your professional framer will also know about conservation framing, which is a method of framing that does not harm the textile. Some cardboards, mats, and wood frames contain acids that over time actually eat away the fabric and thread fibers. Always specify acid-free materials.

Another caveat—whether you frame a piece yourself or have it framed, make sure that the glass does not sit directly on the embroidery—a mat ensures some space between the embroidery and the glass and eliminates the trapping of moisture.

Check out several framers in your area, and ask other needleworkers whom they use before committing to a particular shop. Costs for framing will vary drastically, as will the level of service and professionalism.

Getting It on the Wall

Displaying and hanging your work on walls can be a daunting decorating task. To help you, I've gathered the following "Lucky 7" guidelines for hanging and grouping pictures that have different sizes, styles, and mats. These guidelines will help your pictures get the attention they deserve and produce the best effect for your room.

1. Unify a mismatched collection of prints by using the same mat and frame for each.

2. Group pictures together instead of scattering them around the room.

3. Hang several small, identical frames close together to make one large "picture" over a sofa.

4. For symmetrical arrangements, hang similar sizes and frames either vertically or horizontally.

5. For asymmetrical arrangements, place the largest picture to one side and arrange the smaller ones together on the other side to balance out the display.

6. Don't hang pictures too high or too low! Consider the proportions of the picture and the wall surface area as well as the surrounding furniture.

7. To make walls look wider and longer, arrange pictures horizontally. To make walls look higher, arrange pictures vertically.

In the Wash

All embroideries will need to be cleaned because dust and dirt are the true enemies of any textile. Even though you might think that your piece is absolutely clean because you see no visible spots or stains, you still need to clean it. Oil stains from your hands and dust from the environment are invisible now but will be apparent years later, especially on cotton pieces. By removing the oil and dust, you help to ensure a long life for your beautiful piece. Of course, if your embroidery is old and valuable, you should not clean it at home but take it to a dry cleaning specialist.

Before washing any embroidery, don't forget the colorfast test we spoke of earlier. Press a wet ball of cotton to threads to see if any dye runs into it. (Reds and purples are particularly susceptible to running.) If you see color on the cotton ball, do not wash the embroidery. (See the tips given later in the chapter for cleaning stains without washing.)

Place some pure soap flakes or mild detergent for delicate fabrics in your sink or in a bucket, and wash the piece gently by hand without rubbing. Orvus is a concentrated biodegradable quilt "soap," available in quilt stores, with no phosphorus—and no soap in it. It is perfect for delicate embroideries. Rinse your embroideries several times in lukewarm water until the water is clear. For the last rinse, use cold water. Use distilled water for the last rinse if you have iron in your water; if you don't, rust stains will show up years later.

If your embroidery has specific stains that may need special treatment, check the following list before attempting to clean them.

Some pieces may not be washable. They may need spot-cleaning instead of being immersed in water. Here are some alternatives to washing:

➤ **Vacuum.** Clean embroideries with a vacuum if they are dusty. Use the nozzle attachment. Often it is recommended that you place a soft nylon screen over the stitching (test a section so screen will not snag stitches) and then move the nozzle back and forth over the screen to protect the stitching. Although you should not brush your embroideries, you may use a soft sable paintbrush to remove dust in raised stitching.

➤ **Dry clean.** Large and valuable embroideries such as wall hangings, upholstered pieces, those with a lot of raised work, or pieces having bad stains should be dry cleaned and not washed. Of course, those items that do not pass the colorfast test will also need to be dry cleaned to prevent the dye in the threads or fabric from running. Be sure to choose a reputable cleaner.

➤ **Sable paintbrush method.** Embroidery having stitching that is "raised" from the cloth is delicate, as is embroidery having metal threads, such as gold or silver. Use a sable paintbrush to very gently stroke in and out of crevices that may have collected dust or dirt.

A Stitch in Time

Do your embroidered napkins or tablecloths have candle wax on them? If the wax is still soft, harden it with an ice cube. Now gently scrape away the wax with a dull knife. Be careful not to damage any of the stitches. Then lay the embroidery face down between two sheets of blotting paper. Press a warm iron over the surface of the paper, letting the wax soak into the paper. If the candles were colored and left a stain, try dipping a sponge in alcohol and blotting up the color, but only after the wax has been removed.

Decorator's Do's and Don'ts

Don't pass by unfinished embroideries at tag sales! They are some of my best finds and only a few dollars. They usually come with appropriate thread to finish them. If they need cleaning, refer to the cleaning tips in this chapter.

Keep Away, Moths!

Take care when storing your embroideries. Bugs, moths, and mildew can cause irreversible damage to textiles. Moths love wool and will make holes in fabrics that are improperly stored. And of course moisture causes mildew, which turns fabrics black with rot.

When your embroideries are not in use, store them wrapped in acid-free paper and in a dark place off the floor. Lay them flat to avoid creases that form after time. If a piece cannot be laid flat, roll it in acid-free tissue paper. Most people like plastic bags for storing things, but plastic bags are not recommended for permanent storage because the plastic gives off a gas harmful to textiles, plus moisture could get in the bag and bring on the mildew. However, you can mitigate the effects by punching some small holes in the plastic or by sealing the bag loosely. My friend Diane uses clean, old pillowcases to store her needlework. Check periodically for moths and mildew. It is also a good idea to clean your embroideries every once in a while.

The Least You Need to Know

➤ Make the planning and stitching of your needlework projects efficient and easy by keeping an embroidery basket or bag handy for all your needles, threads, and fabrics, plus the basic tools needed to finish your work.

➤ Learning the art of mounting and blocking will help you finish your embroideries with a professional look.

➤ Selecting frames for your finished work requires a good sense of design and scale. Hanging embroideries in different groupings and mixing with other art can heighten the impact of your work.

➤ Learning to clean, care, and store your embroideries properly will preserve your work for generations.

Chapter 10

An Easy Embroidery Project from Start to Finish

In This Chapter

➤ Stitching your ABCs—a sampler

➤ Preparation is the best way to start any project

➤ Use graphs to design your own samplers

As a novice, it's good to start with small projects that are quickly completed. Not everyone is ready to stitch The Declaration of Independence! I recommend beginning with a small cross stitch sampler to practice your letters, and then framing it to hang on your wall.

In this chapter you will proceed step by step, from the materials needed to get started to advice on finishing your sampler, with plenty of helpful hints along the way. You will embroider the alphabet and numbers and a couple of stars! There is nothing quite as comforting as a charming sampler framed as wall decor to be treasured for generations to come.

Now's the time to take all the information you learned in the previous chapters and put it to work, actually performing the skills of embroidery. Clear instructions will make your first endeavor painless and fun! Just think how proud of your completed project you will be. Now remember to go step by step, take your time, and finish your sampler.

Small, Simple and Sweet: A Sampler

The sampler, as you may recall from Chapter 6, "Initially Speaking: The Art of Monogramming," was used in the past to teach children the alphabet and numerals. This is a perfect choice for a first embroidery project, since you can get acquainted with your materials as well as learn the ins and outs of stitching letters and numbers. This practice comes in handy when you want to sign and date your pieces. Let's start with a very simple sampler that showcases the alphabet in uppercase as well as lowercase and the numbers 1 through 10, with some star motifs for variety.

Getting Acquainted with the Materials

A good way to begin a new craft is to collect all the necessary materials and then try them out ... see how the thread works with the needle and fabric. Here is the list of materials that you will need to stitch the small sampler project. You can purchase them at your local stitchery shop or at a large chain store like Wal-Mart.

➤ 12-inch × 12-inch 14-count Aida cloth in ivory

➤ DMC Six Stranded Embroidery Cotton (347), dark salmon

➤ No. 26 tapestry needle

➤ Embroidery hoop, 9-inch

➤ Pencil, ruler

➤ Cotton thread for basting (different color than above)

➤ Embroidery scissors, 3- or 4-inch

The Fabric

For your sampler, you will be using *Aida cloth*. Aida is a sturdy cotton fabric woven in such a way that small squares are formed, producing a gridlike effect. One cross stitch is placed in each square, and a tiny hole at each corner makes it clear where the needle comes up and goes down. Since this particular size of Aida cloth is woven so that there are 14 holes, or squares, per inch, it is called 14-count Aida.

The Needle

As you learned in Chapter 3, "Tools of the Trade," for every project there is a particular needle used that works with the thread and type of fabric.

The needle for this project is a *tapestry* needle, rather than a sharp-tipped needle. Because of its blunt tip, the tapestry needle will slip through the holes in the Aida fabric without piercing it, as a sharp-tipped needle would. The size that you will use in this project is a number 26.

The Thread

The thread used for this cross-stitch project is DMC Six Stranded Embroidery Floss, a high-quality mercerized cotton floss. If you look at the cut end of the floss, you can clearly see the six separate strands that are gently twisted to create the floss. To cross stitch on 14-count Aida cloth, you will work with only two of the six strands. Pull a length of thread from the skein (pull from the label end) and separate out, or "strip," the two strands. This produces a fuller-looking stitch because the stripped strands lie side by side when recombined.

Clever Crafter

The earliest surviving dated sampler was stitched by Jane Bostocke in 1598, and it now resides in the Victoria and Albert Museum in London.

Helpful Tools

In your basket you should have a hoop to mount your cloth on. This will help keep your sampler fabric taut and clean. Use your pencil to mark the arrow for the center points on the chart. The basting thread should be used to mark the center vertical and horizontal points of the fabric. If these tools are always kept in your embroidery basket, it makes your projects so much easier to start and complete.

Reading the Chart

The chart is illustrated on graph paper using a symbol to guide you. This sampler is done in one color for ease and style. Each symbol—a small cross—represents a stitch on the chart. Each square on the chart represents one square on the fabric. The symbols on the chart show where the stitches go and also represent the color to be used for the stitch. By embroidering cross stitches in the corresponding squares of the Aida cloth, you will be able to make your sampler come to life! Be sure to mark the vertical and horizontal midpoints with an arrow so that you can find the center of the chart.

The Stitch

You will use the cross stitch on this sampler as illustrated in Chapter 5, "In Stitches." Refer to the diagram and instructions for any help on how to work the basic cross stitch. It is one of the easiest to master.

Preparing Your Thread

1. First cut the embroidery floss into lengths of approximately 18 inches. You will find this to be an easy length to work with.

2. Pull the thread from the label end of the skein (it pulls easier from that end). Keep holding onto the label end of the thread and cut off the desired length.

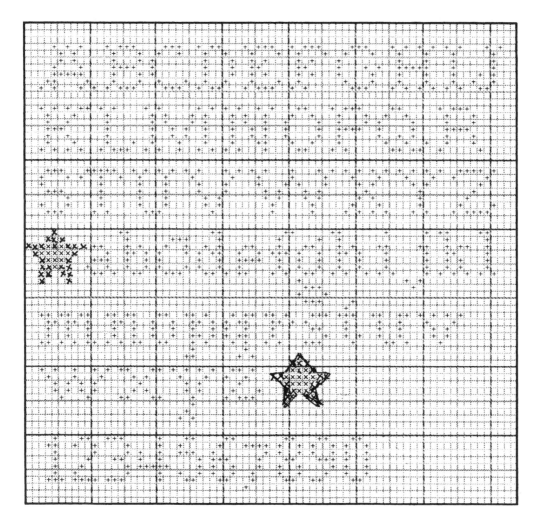

3. Hold that end in your right hand, near the top of the thread. With your left hand, tap the top several times. You will see that the strands fluff out and separate (sometimes called "blooming"). Now you can easily select a strand to pull. Pull a single strand straight up with your left hand while firmly holding the remainder of the length with your right.

4. After the strand has been pulled out, give the length in your right hand a shake. The remaining strands will fall smoothly back in place. If the strands bunch up instead of falling free, you are holding the wrong end. Simply turn the length of thread upside down and tap again.

5. Continue to pull out as many strands as you need, one by one. Recombine the appropriate number (two for this sampler).

6. Note that the end you tapped is also the end that is threaded into the needle. Orienting the thread this way keeps the thread from snarling as you pull it through the fabric. This method is almost foolproof.

If the floss becomes tightly twisted while embroidering, drop the needle and let it hang. The floss will untwist by itself. Tightly twisted floss appears thin and will not cover the fabric.

Thread your needle with the two strands of floss.

Decorator's Do's and Don'ts

Never knot your thread! Leave a one-inch tail of thread at the back of the fabric. Hold the tail with your finger and proceed to make your stitches so that they cover the tail on the back. The stitches will anchor the tail.

Preparing Your Fabric

1. Turn under and sew, serge, or zigzag the edges of the fabric to prevent fraying.

2. Find the center of your fabric by folding the fabric in half, and in half again, and creasing lightly.

3. Baste along both fold lines—where the two lines cross is the center reference point. These lines will guide you when following the chart.

4. After each stitching session, be sure to remove the embroidery hoop. If left in place, it eventually leaves a permanent crease (it actually breaks the fibers) on the fabric. Refer to Chapter 3 to refresh your memory on how to use the hoop.

Ready, Set, Stitch

1. Thread your needle with two strands of thread.

2. Find the center point of the chart. Start your cross stitch (see Chapter 5 to review) at the top left corner of chart.

3. Measure the inches from the top-left corner and from the left edge of the fabric to where the finished design will be centered.

4. From that point count over to the first stitch to begin. Use your chart as your guide—remember that each symbol on the graph represents one cross stitch on your fabric.

5. Count your stitches frequently to eliminate the chances of making a mistake.

Framing

When you have completed the sampler, you should frame it so that you can show the world your first stab at embroidery! Refer to Chapter 9, "The Embroiderer's Finishing Touch," for blocking and mounting your sampler. The finished size of this sampler should be 9 × 9 inches. An antique frame will give your work instant age and heritage. A sleek frame, such as a piece of glass with clips, will show off the edges of the sampler, a combination of traditional and modern.

Clever Crafter

To give an instant aged appearance to your sampler, dip the fabric in a coffee or tea solution. To a quart of boiling water, add six teaspoons of instant coffee or tea leaves. Bring to a boil and remove from heat. Dip your sampler in cold water and then in the hot solution for one minute. Place on an absorbent cloth and iron by placing a clean cloth on top of your stitching. Always make sure your materials are colorfast! I like to do this after stitching so the entire piece has the aged effect.

Grids to Make Your Own

After you complete your sampler, you may want to design your own sampler, or perhaps you have a different type of design in mind that you just can't wait to start stitching. Strike out on your own and use the graph paper provided in this chapter to sketch your own patterns and designs. Feel free to photocopy these sheets if you need more paper.

Decorator's Do's and Don'ts

Don't jump too far from one area to another. Threads that run across the back of the embroidery, especially dark colors, will show through on the front. Finish one area; then start again. For example, the basic rule for 14-count would be to carry the thread no more than four squares. Sometimes it's possible to run the thread under previous stitches and perhaps carry it five or six stitches, but no more than that.

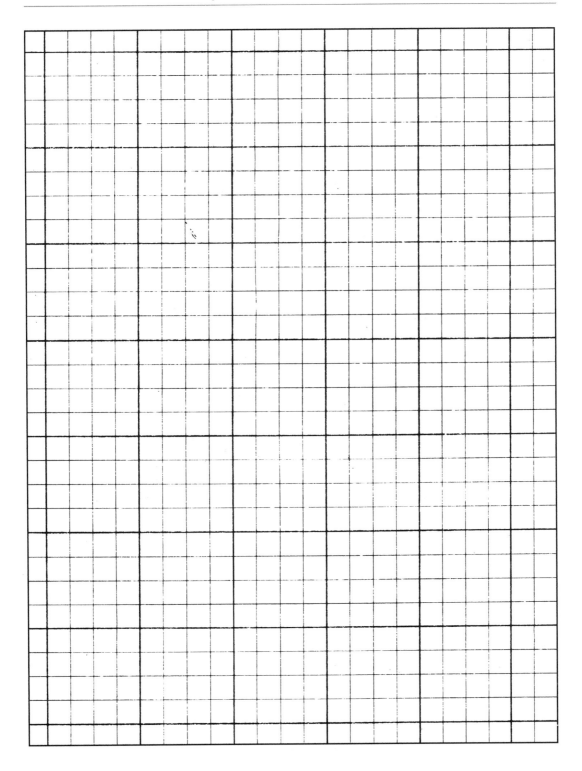

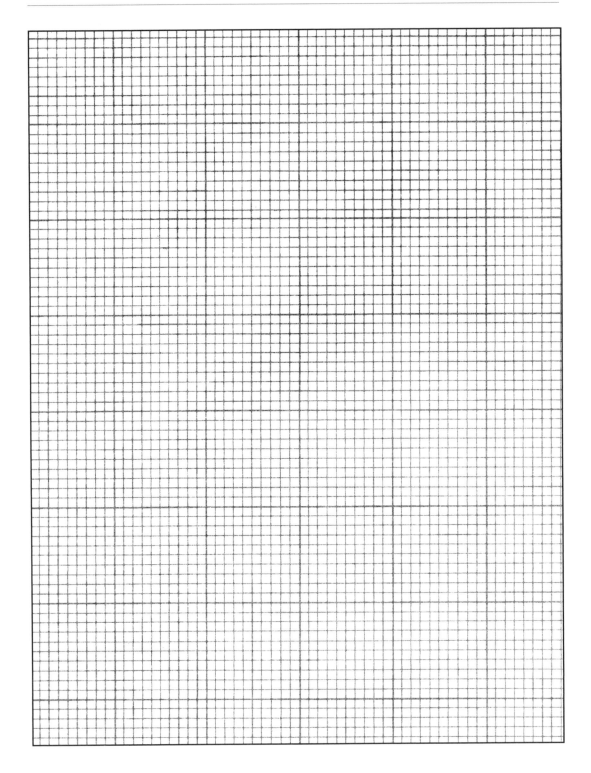

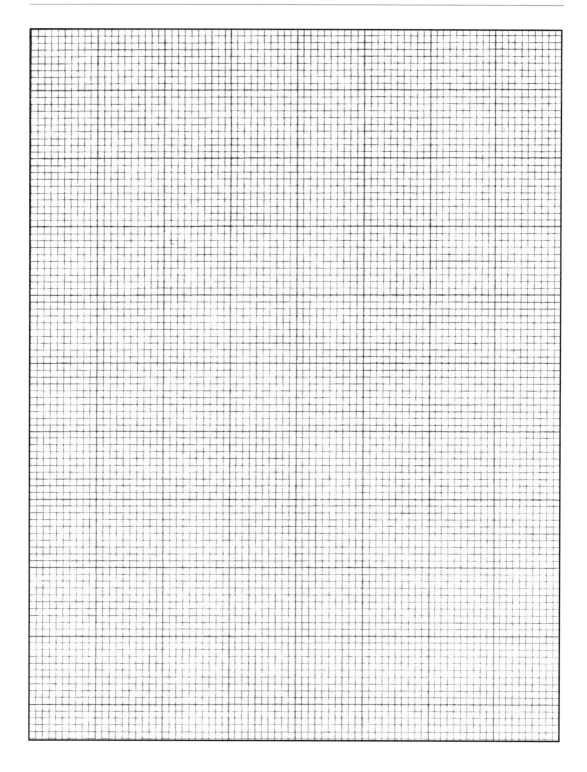

The Least You Need to Know

➤ Small projects are a good beginning for novices. A sampler is a good choice.

➤ A good way to start a new craft is to get a feel for your materials ... how the thread works with the needle and fabric.

➤ Preparing your threads and fabric before starting makes a project easier.

➤ Graph paper is great for drawing your own designs.

Part 4
Needlepoint Basics

As you learned in Part 1 of this book, needlepoint is actually a form of embroidery. Its stitches are done on heavy canvas and usually made into household goods. Now that you've picked up embroidery, needlepoint will seem relatively easy. It is easier in some ways and just as fun.

Some needlepoint stitches are the same as those found in embroidery. Bargello, however, is unique to needlepoint. With Bargello techniques, you'll create wonderful textures and patterns for items in your home!

Chapter 11

Needlepoint Tools of the Trade

> ## In This Chapter
>
> ➤ Learning the right size and type of canvases
>
> ➤ Knowing your needlepoint needles and the weights of yarns
>
> ➤ Using kits: a beginner's salvation

Welcome to the world of needlepoint! As you may recall from Part 1, "Welcome to Needlecrafts," needlepoint is a type of embroidery that is characterized by the use of *canvas,* a special type of open-weave fabric having a square mesh. Needlepoint is sometimes known as "tapestry," because items stitched with the basic needlepoint stitches (tent, diagonal, and straight) have a woven look that resembles a tapestry wall hanging. Compared with the embroidery stitches that you learned earlier, needlepoint stitches are very easy to learn.

In addition to canvas, needlepoint essentials include needles and yarn, which all must be carefully matched to work together. A frame, as well as other small tools, can make needlepoint easier. Color-coordinated kits with all these items prepackaged may be the simplest way to start.

Your Canvas

As in painting, needlepoint uses a "canvas" to work on. Unlike painting, however, the needlepoint canvas is not made from canvas at all. Most needlepoint canvases are made from cotton or linen. They are *mesh* fabrics with criss-crossing fibers that form a grid. The open spaces allow the needle and yarn to pass through to form the needle-point work.

You can purchase canvas by the yard, depending on the size of your design/project. It comes in basic colors of antique brown, white, and cream, which are suitable for most applications; as well as a variety of specialty colors, such as black, sage, peach, and pale blue.

Besides having a choice of color, you have a choice of mesh size. The mesh size, or gauge, is determined by the number of threads per inch. The higher the number, the finer the canvas, and vice versa—the lower the number, the coarser the canvas. For example, very detailed work may require a fine-gauge canvas of 22 threads per inch, whereas a rug will require thick rug canvas with a gauge of 3 threads per inch. A common gauge used in needlepoint is 10, which you now know means 10 threads per inch.

Needlework 101

Mesh is any fabric of open texture having a netlike quality.

Mono Canvas

Mono canvas is sold in the largest range of gauges. It consists of single threads that form a grid. When you learn about needlepoint stitches in Chapter 13, "Just Point and Stitch," you will find out that mono canvas is not suitable for working half and cross stitches.

Mono canvas comes in the widest range of gauges.

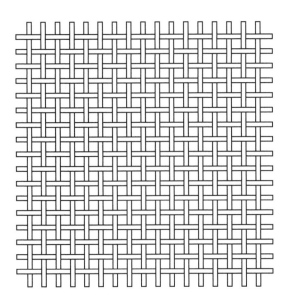

Double or Penelope Canvas

The *double*, or "Penelope," canvas is made with pairs of horizontal and vertical threads. You can work your stitches over each pair or split them for smaller stitches when you need more detail. This is sometimes referred to as "pricking the ground."

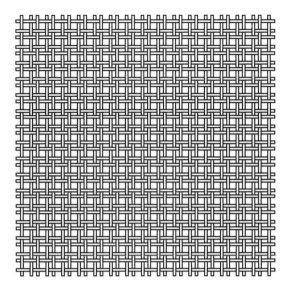

In double, or Penelope, canvas, the threads can be split for smaller stitches or can be worked in pairs.

Interlock and Rug Canvases

Other types of canvases are interlock and rug, used for wall hangings and rugs. *Interlock* canvas is made of pairs of twisted vertical threads that intersect single horizontal threads. This weave makes interlock less likely to distort or fray.

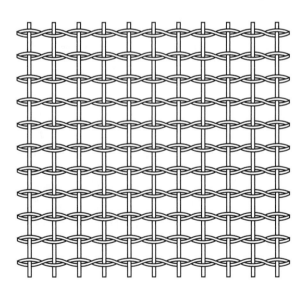

Interlock canvas is less likely to distort during stitching.

Rug canvas is a sturdy canvas used for needlepoint and rug making. It is formed by two lengthwise threads that are twisted around each other and a pair of crosswise

115

threads. The threads cannot be separated. Rug canvas comes in three to five gauges and is used primarily for rugs.

Rug canvas has interlock-ing construction to give it shape.

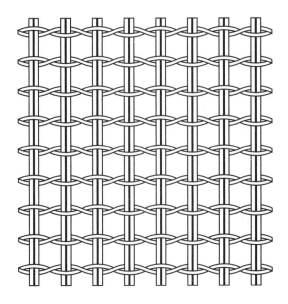

Plastic and Paper Canvas

Plastic canvas is a molded, rather than woven, canvas-looking material that comes in precut sheets with a medium gauge. It is typically used for place mats, cards, and craft decorations such as ornaments. Plastic canvas has a stiff feel and is not recommended for fine needlework.

Plastic and paper canvas is used for "crafty" items like place mats, cards, and decorations.

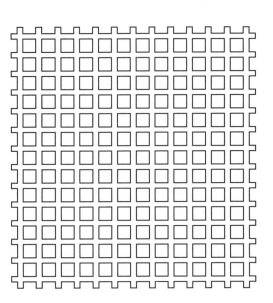

Fourteen-count perforated paper, available in ecru, brown, and other colors (sometimes gold, silver, and red) is a stiff, heavy paper that has been coated for durability. It is suitable for both needlepoint and cross stitch decorations and cards.

To the Point: Needles

Tapestry needles are specifically used for needlepoint. They have blunt ends to protect the thread and canvas from being split during stitching. Their large eyes make it easy to thread heavier weights of yarn. They are available in various sizes ranging from 28, the smallest, to 13, the largest. The smaller sizes are primarily used in cross stitch, and the larger ones in needlepoint, with size 24 being used for both. A size 18 needle is suitable for 10- and 12-mesh canvas. Be sure you select a size that fits the mesh holes of your canvas without distorting them.

> **A Stitch in Time**
>
> It is very important to choose the right needle. The needle and yarn should pass easily through the canvas. A kit will include the correct size yarn and needle, or a specialty shop owner can advise you.

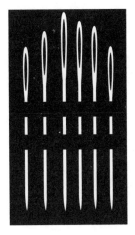

Tapestry needles are fashioned with blunt ends and large round eyes for easy threading.

Yarn

There are three types of wool yarn manufactured for needlepoint: crewel, tapestry, and Persian. They are colorfast, durable, and available in many beautiful shades. Other yarns tailored for more specific types of projects include rug wool, crochet, embroidery cottons, silk floss, and metallic threads.

Crewel is the finest of the wool needlepoint yarns, a little finer than Persian yarn. It can be worked in a single strand on a very fine mesh canvas, or two, three, or four strands can be combined for coarser work.

Decorator's Do's and Don'ts

If you work with dark-color yarns, don't choose a white canvas. Select brown canvas so that any gaps in your stitching won't be noticeable and spoil your design.

Persian wool is made up of three easily divided strands. These strands can be separated to suit the gauge of your canvas.

Tapestry wool is a single strand yarn, a bit finer than three strands of Persian wool. It is usually used with medium-gauge canvas.

Rug wool is a very thick, long-lasting, single-strand yarn.

All four types of yarn are available in a man-made fiber—acrylic—which is less expensive and easier to wash, but not as handsome for heirloom projects.

Crochet or embroidery cottons, silks, and metal threads can be used alone or in conjunction with other threads for outlining or accents.

Yarns pictured from top to bottom are crewel, tapestry, and Persian.

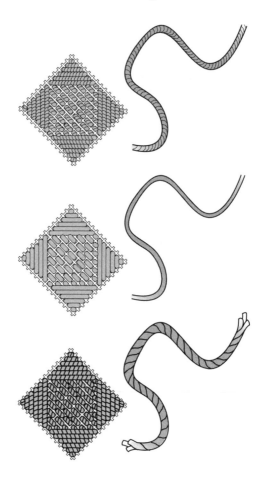

Frames

Although frames aren't absolutely necessary for working a needlepoint design, they are helpful for keeping the canvas stretched evenly and for preventing distortion. If the frame is supported by a stand, then both of your hands can be free. The flat straight-sided frame works best for canvas. An adjustable straight frame on a stand is best for large pieces of canvas. Refresh your memory by reading the section on frames in Chapter 3, "Tools of the Trade."

The Little Extras

Good results in needlework come from using good-quality implements. Along with the right needles and threads, fill your needlepoint bag or basket with the following:

➤ **Embroidery scissors.** Find a pair that is sharp, light, pointed, and small (three to four inches long). Blunt-tipped scissors, like those sold for children, aren't suitable.

➤ **Dressmaker shears.** These are best for cutting fabric. If you use them to cut canvas, be aware that over time they will become dull from the rough canvas threads.

➤ **Felt-tip marker.** Markers are great for drawing designs on fabric. Stock up on waterproof-type only in lots of colors.

➤ **Masking tape.** Use tape to bind the edges of the canvas to prevent raveling and to keep the edges from snagging your yarn.

➤ **Dressmaker's carbon paper.** Use it to transfer designs to canvas.

➤ **Acrylic paints.** These paints are good for painting designs or for changing a color on a preprinted design.

➤ **Paintbrush.** If you decide to paint your own canvases, you will need to invest in an acrylic paintbrush.

Needlepoint ... Ready to Go

Just as in the fashion world of ready-to-wear clothing, there is ready-to-do needlepoint in the needlework world. It is the quickest way to get going on a project, when the canvas already is preprinted with a design and materials are specified or prepackaged. Read on to see the possibilities and best choice for you.

Kits

Needlepoint kits are great for the beginner because they already have the right needle, the proper amount and weight of yarn in the specified colors, and the correct gauge of canvas. What could be easier! The design is usually printed on the canvas or in chart form included in the kit. The chart will be a graph, like the graph in the last chapter, in which each square will represent a stitch.

Hand-Painted Designs

Canvases having hand-painted designs are another option. These may be one-of-a-kind or limited-production designs. You select and buy your own yarn to match the colors of the paint, although some canvases come with the matching colored yarn. A specialty shop owner can recommend the proper yarn and amounts of each color.

Charts

Charted designs have squares that represent a stitch. The squares are marked with colored inks or with symbols, defined in a key at the side of the chart. The charts are printed on paper and the canvas is blank. By measuring and counting meshes and using the color chart on the paper as a guide, you can begin stitching. Each square on the paper represents a color and type of stitch.

Trammed Canvas

Some canvases come with long, horizontal stitches, called *tramé,* run across the design. Diagonal stitches are then worked over the horizontal stitches to add thickness and strength to the canvas. Pieces that will get a lot of wear, like seat or footstool covers, are often trammed.

Stored but Ready to Go

As in embroidery and any craft, the best workers have their tools ready to go. Baskets work well for needlepoint yarn and canvas. Keep your needles in plastic containers or in a needle case (available at stitching shops) to avoid losing them. Try to keep your yarns neat—and away from your cat!

The Least You Need to Know

➤ Needlepoint requires only a few tools and is easy to pick up.

➤ Needlepoint canvases come in many different gauges that require the appropriate-sized needle and weight of yarn.

➤ Tapestry needles are required for needlepoint because of their blunt ends and large eyes.

➤ Yarns come in many different colors and weights. They must be selected to work with the right needle and canvas.

➤ Kits are the easiest way to begin doing needlepoint.

Needlepoint Tips and Tricks

Before you grab that canvas, needle, and thread for your first stab at needlepoint, you'll want to read some of the techniques in this chapter that will make needlepoint easier, neater, and fun! Although needlepoint is a breeze to pick up, you'll find that by learning some stitching tips, and the basics of handling the canvas, starting your design, and finishing off your work, your project will be that much easier and satisfying.

As in embroidery, don't forget to keep your eye out for ideas. Keep gathering projects, and remember to store them in one easy-to-reach place, such as a file cabinet or basket close at hand. This will keep you stitching every day!

You may want to copy some of your filed patterns by using the various transfer techniques covered in this chapter. To keep these techniques close by, I suggest photocopying the section on transferring, as well as the one in Chapter 4, "Technique Chic," and adding these pages to your project box. Looking for projects to transfer? Get more project ideas in Chapter 2, "Well-Designed Needle Art."

Fragile ... Handle with Care!

Older canvas materials tended to fray easily. Although today's canvases don't fray nearly as much, it is still a good idea to place masking tape neatly around the edges, especially if you will be handling the project for a length of time (usually the case with large canvases or those you carry around a lot). Taping will keep the edges of your canvas neat and clean.

Masking tape will keep the edges of your canvas from fraying.

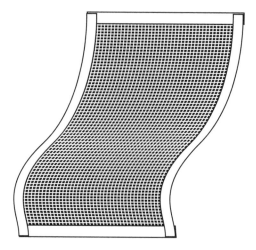

If your canvas is very large, try rolling it up to the section you are working on and securing with clothespins to make it less cumbersome to work with. Be sure to roll upward with the design on the inside.

Before blocking your needlepoint projects, be sure to make a paper template of the original size and shape of your canvas so that when you do reshape it you will have a guide to go by. As you learned in embroidery (Chapter 9, "The Embroiderer's Finishing Touch"), you will need to block your finished needlepoint to return it to its original shape. An easy way to view the original size (for small designs) is to photocopy it at full size.

Take a Stab at Stitches

There are two methods of stitching in needlepoint: the stabbing method and the sewing method. The stabbing method requires two movements to make a stitch and is easier to use with a frame. The sewing method requires one movement. Either method may be used for hand-held needlepoint. See which one works for you!

For the *stabbing method,* it requires two movements for each stitch. Insert the needle into your canvas from the back side through to the right side of the canvas at the point where stitch is to be formed. Then the needle and yarn are pulled through to the back side of the canvas.

Decorator's Do's and Don'ts

Don't use yarn that's too thin! Use a proper thickness that will cover your canvas and prevent the mesh from showing. A good way to test which yarn is right for your project is to stitch a sample section. If the yarn is too thin, add another strand or two until the mesh is covered. If it's difficult to pull the thread through the canvas or if the canvas seems to ripple, decrease the number of strands.

The stabbing method.

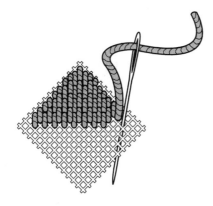

The *sewing method* requires one motion: The needle is inserted into the canvas from the right side of your canvas and brought out at the point where the next stitch is to be formed. Pull the thread through to the front.

The sewing method.

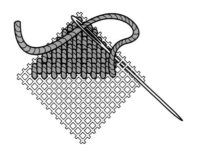

123

Thread Tech

The following tips about threads and yarns will help you keep frustrations at bay and your needlepoint looking its best.

Points to remember:

➤ If the thread begins to twist or tangle, let it drop down from the canvas and unwind before you continue.

➤ Begin with a working thread of 18 inches to prevent fraying as it is worked through the canvas.

➤ Do not start and end new threads at the same point. The thickness of the threads will cause a bumpy ridge that will be visible from the right side of your work.

Leave at least an inch of thread at the back. Work a few stitches over it to secure it. Cut off any excess.

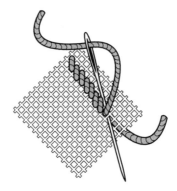

➤ Never start a new thread with a knot. This will also form bumps in your work.

➤ Wool yarn has a right and wrong end. The right end must thread the needle. Run your thumb and forefinger downward along the length of the yarn. If it feels smooth, you have the right end.

Bring the needle through to the back of your work. Weave the thread through the backside of the canvas through the last six to eight stitches. Cut off the excess.

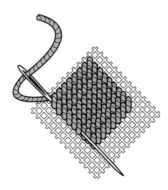

Transferring Techniques

As you learn some of the basic techniques with your needle, canvas, and threads, you may be thinking of some patterns that you would like to borrow and turn into a needlepoint. You can transfer a pattern or your drawing with one of the following methods.

Using Dressmaker's Carbon

The dressmaker's carbon paper method is ideal if you are using a fine-gauge canvas. With tracing paper, copy the original pattern or drawing. Then place a sheet of dressmaker's carbon between the tracing and the canvas and retrace the outline. The pattern will show up on the canvas.

The Homemade Light Box Trick

To transfer a picture or pattern that you already have, try using a homemade light box. This method is actually simple to do, and the transfer is easy. Place a sheet of glass between two chairs (or use a glass tabletop), and put a lamp with high wattage underneath it. Now place the drawing or pattern on top of the glass and the canvas on top of the drawing. The light will pass through both pieces so you can easily follow the outline of the drawing.

You can also simply hold your pattern up to a window for a similar effect.

Use a fine felt-tip waterproof pen to mark the design on the canvas. Referring to the original pattern as a guide, mark the colors you will use for the needlepoint stitches on the canvas. Use acrylic paints or felt-tip markers to color in the design.

Decorator's Do's and Don'ts

Don't use plain carbon paper for transferring your designs. Regular carbon will ruin your fabric. Use dressmaker's carbon only.

A Stitch in Time

It's a good idea to buy only the waterproof-type markers for your "tool kit." That way, when you block your needlepoint, you'll be sure that the marker colors won't run.

Transferring with Markers and Paints

If you are creating a design from scratch, first make a rough sketch of it on paper. Don't re-create it on your canvas just yet. Practice a few sketches—don't skip this step unless you're a solid artist. Later, when you actually transfer your design to canvas, you'll be glad you tried it out on paper first!

When you're happy with your practice run, draw your design in full scale and color it in with markers. Draw a square (or rectangle) outline around the outer edges of the pattern. Divide the design into even quarters by drawing one horizontal and one vertical line intersecting at the center point. This will be useful for transferring your design with paints as well as for charting your design.

Cut your canvas with a three-inch border all around. Mark the top of the canvas with a fine waterproof felt-tip marker. Draw lines on the canvas dividing the canvas into even quarters. Place the canvas over the drawing, and match up the center lines that you just drew. Tape down the corners of the canvas, and draw the outer edges of the design onto the canvas with a waterproof felt-tip pen.

Remove the tape from the corners, and lift the canvas from the design.

You can now paint the design with colors, using your original drawing design as a guide. Let the canvas completely dry before starting your needlepoint.

Charting a Design

Charting a design on graph paper will allow you to work out the design on canvas with accurate details. Mark the center point of the graph paper and, referring to your original sketch, use the center points to chart your design on the graph paper. On the graph paper, mark each square of the design in the appropriate color until your design is charted. Remember that each square represents one stitch, and each stitch is worked over one intersection of the canvas.

Now that you know the basic techniques of needlepoint, it's time that you learn the stitches, and that is the topic of the next chapter. Soon you will be stitching your first needlepoint project.

Decorator's Do's and Don'ts

Don't assume that your graph paper is the same scale as your canvas. For example, your charted or graphed flower that is six inches in height on the graph paper may be much smaller on the canvas. To figure the finished design size, count the number of squares on the graph (length and width) and divide by the gauge of the canvas. Consider this when planning your design. Stitch a sample of a part of your pattern to assess the scale.

The Least You Need to Know

➤ Canvases should be handled with care! Bind the edges with masking tape to prevent fraying.

➤ There are two methods of stitching: the sewing and the stabbing method. Both are fine for hand-held canvases, but the stabbing method is better for canvases that are in a frame.

➤ By using the correct techniques for starting and ending your thread or yarn, you avoid getting ridges and bumps in your work.

➤ There are several ways to transfer your favorite pattern to needlepoint canvas: using dressmaker's carbon, a light box, paints and markers, and graph paper.

Chapter 13

Just Point and Stitch

In This Chapter

➤ Getting the hang of needlepoint by learning tent and other diagonal stitches

➤ Trying out the basic and not-so-basic crossed and straight stitches

➤ Fancying up your designs with star and loop stitches

With the right tools and some basic techniques, you can move ahead and learn all of the many needlepoint stitches that will make your designs come alive with texture and personality. In needlepoint, simply by changing directions with some stitches and combining others, your designs can take on fabulous looks. Experiment with the stitches in this book by working a sampler of the stitches for reference and practice.

I've included a sampling of needlepoint's basic stitches in this chapter. Over time, you will discover that you like to do certain stitches more than others and these will become your own "basic" stitches.

The following instructions for tent, diagonal, crossed, straight, starred, and looped stitches state the number of canvas threads over which the stitches should be worked in each direction. After you get the hang of the basic version of each stitch, you can vary the length of the stitch depending on the effect you want to achieve. Keep in mind one of the biggest rules in needlepoint: Never work stitches over more than 10 canvas threads. The loops of long stitches are liable to snag. All of the needlepoint stitches in this chapter are worked on either mono or double canvas.

Tent

Tent stitches are small diagonal stitches that are worked in the same direction over one *intersection* of canvas. There are three variations: the half-cross stitch, the continental stitch, and the basketweave stitch. The half-cross stitch is the easiest to execute and uses the least amount of yarn. It is also the least durable. It cannot be used on mono canvas because the stitches tend to slip.

Both the half-cross stitch and continental stitch tend to distort the canvas, so using a frame is a good idea if you are working a large area. The basketweave stitch does not distort the canvas. However, it uses more yarn than the half-cross stitch and continental stitches.

Needlework 101

Intersection in needlepoint refers to the point at which a horizontal and a vertical canvas thread meet.

Half-Cross Stitch

The *half-cross* stitch is worked in horizontal rows from left to right. To begin, bring the needle through to the front of the canvas. Now take it diagonally up to the right and over one horizontal thread, pulling through to the back, as shown in the next figure. Bring your needle up again, ready to make the next stitch.

The half-cross stitch is a popular needlepoint stitch used for fillings, backgrounds, and outlines.

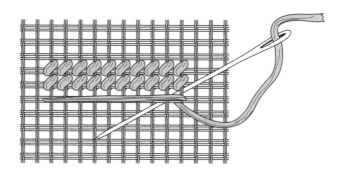

When you complete the first row, turn your canvas upside down to start the next row in the same manner. Repeat by bringing your needle up and taking it down at the first intersection to the right.

Continental Stitch

The *continental* stitch is worked in rows from right to left, just the opposite of the half-cross.

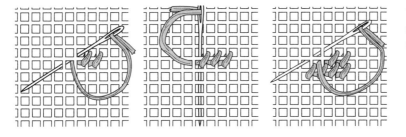

The continental stitch can be used on single canvas.

To start, bring the needle through to the front of the canvas and take it diagonally up and over one canvas intersection to the right. Then take the needle diagonally under one intersection to the left.

At the end of the row, turn your canvas upside down for the return row.

Basketweave Stitch

You guessed it—the *basketweave* stitch resembles the weave of a basket on the back side of the canvas. This stitch is excellent for upholstery pieces that receive wear, such as seat covers and piano bench covers, because the large amount of yarn on the back side protects the canvas.

Needlework 101

Petit point, meaning "small stitch," is the French term for tent stitch.

Basketweave is the perfect stitch to work over large areas because it won't distort the canvas.

For this stitch, you will work up and down the canvas in a diagonal pattern. First, take a stitch up to the right over one intersection and insert your needle down under two horizontal canvas threads.

Diagonal

The tent stitch is a diagonal stitch formed over one canvas mesh and is a diagonal stitch that produces an even texture that is applicable to any type of needlepoint design. The following diagonal stitches are formed over two canvas meshes and are

131

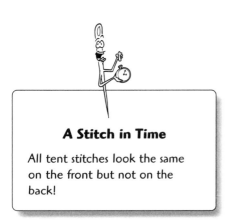

stitched in a slanted direction over the canvas threads. The diagonal stitches described in this section—Gobelin, condensed Scottish, checker, and Byzantine—form various patterns, such as checkerboard, zigzag, and stripes, all of which are further emphasized by combining different colors of yarn.

Gobelin Stitch

No, *Gobelin* is not a stitch that was invented by a famous goblin. Rather, the Gobelin stitch (note different spelling from gremlin-like creature) was born in a famous Paris tapestry factory of the same name.

For the Gobelin stitch you'll need to work on single canvas only *because the stitches tend to slip*. This stitch is worked from left to right and alternately from right to left.

The Gobelin stitch is a larger version of petit point.

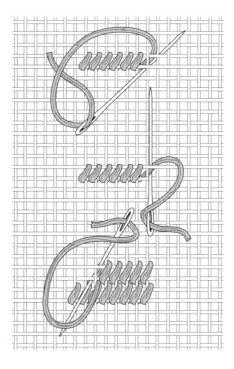

Bring your needle through to the front of the canvas, and insert it two horizontal canvas threads up and one vertical canvas thread to the right. The needle is now at the back of the canvas. Bring the needle to the front, two horizontal threads down and one vertical stitch to the left of the stitch just taken.

In the next row, work new stitches one stitch length below your previous row. Create these stitches in the same slanting direction.

Encroaching Gobelin

The *encroaching Gobelin* stitch is a form of the Gobelin, but the stitches are longer. Work it the same way as the Gobelin stitch, except take each stitch over four (or five) canvas threads, slanting over one vertical thread. On the next rows, overlap the tops of the stitches by one thread.

Needlework 101

Gros point, meaning "large point" in French, is another name for the Gobelin stitch. It is a larger version of the tent stitch.

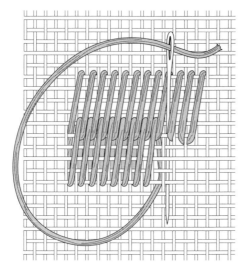

The encroaching Gobelin is a perfect choice for filling large areas and for giving shaded effects.

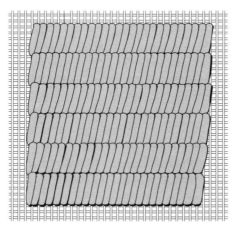

Working Graduated Diagonal Stitches

Graduated diagonal stitches are formed by using different lengths of diagonal stitches, and patterns happen!

The square in the following figure is worked over a graduating number of intersections in the canvas. It is worked in a group of seven stitches over 1, 2, 3, 4, 3, 2, and 1 intersections.

Various patterns can be formed by combining different lengths of diagonal stitches.

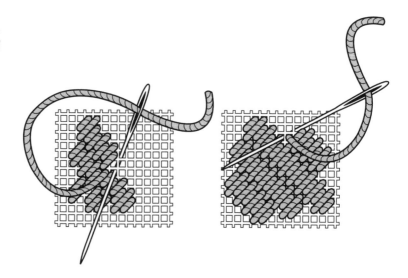

The condensed Scottish stitch, described next, is an example of a graduated diagonal stitch worked in a group of four.

Condensed Scottish Stitch

The *condensed Scottish* stitch is a group of four diagonal stitches worked over 2, 3, 4, and 3 canvas intersections. It is always worked diagonally. Work the graduated stitches in diagonal rows starting at the top right. The basic unit of the pattern is a group of the 4 diagonal stitches that are worked over 2, 3, 4, and 3 canvas intersections. Repeat. Repeat the same stitch sequence for the next row placing the shortest stitch next to the longest stitch of the previous row.

Checker Stitch

Another of the slanted variety, the *checker* stitch is worked in graduated diagonal stitches over four horizontal and four vertical canvas threads.

Begin at the top left. In the first row, fill each square with seven diagonal stitches worked over 1, 2, 3, 4, 3, 2, and 1 intersections (for the stitch pattern, refer to the first figure under the heading "Working Graduated Diagonal Stitches").

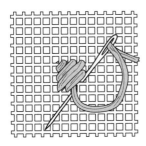
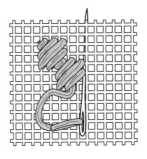

If worked in different colors, the condensed Scottish stitch forms a striped pattern.

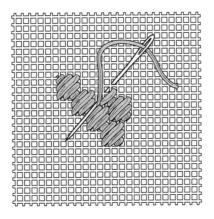

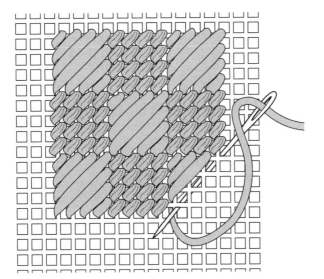

The checker stitch forms—what else?— a checkerboard effect.

In the second row you'll create the "checker" effect by using tent stitches. Work 16 tent stitches (half-cross, continental, or any of your choosing) into each new square. These new squares fit neatly into the previous row's squares.

Byzantine Stitch

The zigzag-style rows of the *Byzantine* stitch are worked diagonally from top to bottom, then in reverse from bottom to top. Work each stitch over two canvas intersections. Start forming your zigzags by making three diagonal stitches across the canvas horizontally and then three diagonal stitches either up or down the canvas (depending on the direction of your design).

The Byzantine stitch is a quick stitch for filling large areas in a zigzag pattern.

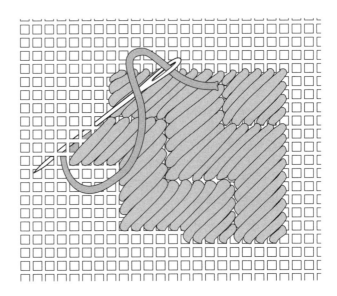

The second set of stitches fits neatly into the preceding row, like a puzzle.

Crossed

The basic *cross* stitch that you learned in the embroidery section of this book will come in very handy for these needlepoint cross stitches. The basic cross stitch is worked on double, or Penelope, canvas only, but other types of cross stitches can be worked on mono canvas. Basic cross stitch can be worked horizontally or diagonally on double canvas. The stitches can go over one or more intersections, depending on the gauge of the canvas. Keep all the top stitches of the crosses lying in the same direction for a neat finish.

Basic Horizontal Cross Stitch

The *horizontal cross* stitch is worked just as it sounds—horizontally. Every row is worked from left to right.

For your first stitch, bring the needle out through the canvas, up to the left, and over two canvas intersections. Insert the needle, bringing it out under two horizontal canvas threads.

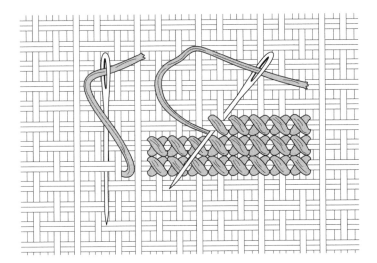

Work horizontal cross stitches from left to right.

Cross this stitch with a diagonal backstitch over the same intersection, but slant it in the opposite direction. Bring the needle out, ready to make the next cross stitch.

Diagonal Cross Stitch

The *diagonal cross* stitch is similar to the horizontal cross stitch. Starting from the bottom left, make your first stitch just like you did in the horizontal method.

Oblong Cross Stitch

The *oblong cross* stitch is worked from right to left and then left to right.

Decorator's Do's and Don'ts

Don't pull too tightly on your diagonal stitches! They tend to distort the canvas more than any other stitch. Do try to use a frame to prevent warping.

Bring out the needle on the front side, and take a stitch up to the left over four horizontal and two vertical canvas threads. Insert the needle and take a stitch under four horizontal threads. Repeat this until the end of the row.

137

Work the diagonal cross stitch from bottom left.

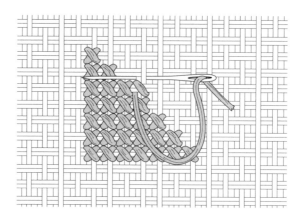

This stitch resembles a series of elongated "X"s.

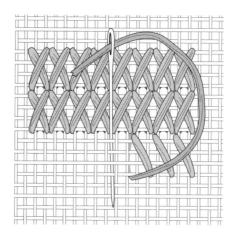

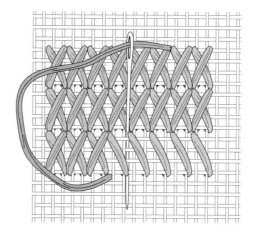

At the end of the first journey, work your way back, crossing with stitches worked in the opposite direction. At the end of the row, bring the needle out four threads down, ready to start the first stitch of the next new row.

Rice Stitch

The *rice* stitch is really a two-step stitch. Bring out the needle at the top left. Stitching horizontally, work a row of large cross stitches over four canvas intersections.

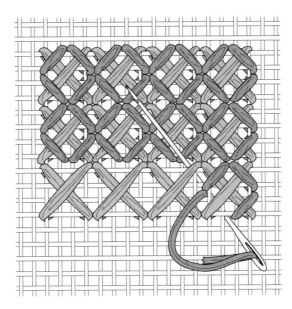

The rice stitch has a doubling "X" effect.

Now, on the return, take a backstitch at right angles and over the center of each cross stitch. Each one of the backstitches covers two canvas intersections. Essentially, you are crossing the "legs" of each larger cross stitch with a smaller stitch.

Work each new row into the base of the stitches from the previous row.

Straight

Straight stitches are easy and quickly stitched. Although not very unique, they can be more interesting if different lengths are combined. Straight stitches are usually worked on single canvas, but double can be used. The following stitches are worked in horizontal rows.

Upright Gobelin Stitch

We're back to the Gobelin stitch but this one is worked in an "upright" fashion. The rows of the *upright Gobelin* are first worked left to right and then right to left.

Bring your needle out *to the front of your canvas,* and insert it up over two horizontal threads and down to the right. Underneath the fabric, move the needle over one vertical and two horizontal threads. Bring your needle out, and start the next stitch the same way.

The upright Gobelin produces a hard-wearing stitch that has a ridged surface.

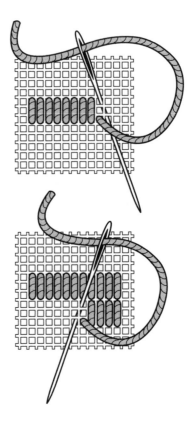

In the next and succeeding rows, work the tops of the stitches into the bases of the previous row.

Gobelin Filling Stitch

Work the first row of the *Gobelin filling* stitch in the same fashion as the upright Gobelin stitch. For the filling stitch, however, work each stitch over six horizontal threads and space them two vertical canvas threads apart. The rows overlap to produce a basketweave effect. This is a good stitch to use just as it states, for filling in areas.

Embroidery and needlepoint make lovely additions to your home décor.

(Laura Ashley)

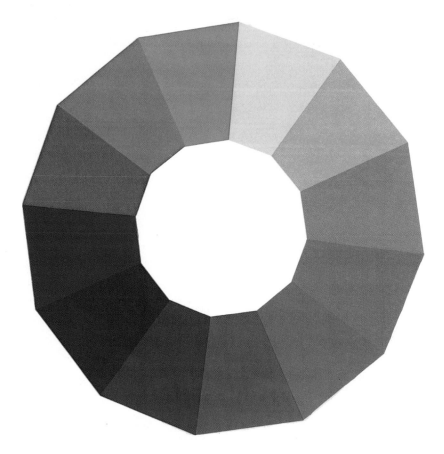

The color wheel is used to select color combinations for needlework.

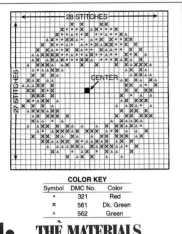

28 STITCHES

CENTER

COLOR KEY

Symbol	DMC No.	Color
•	321	Red
×	561	Dk. Green
▲	562	Green

1. THE MATERIALS

THE CLOTH

Aida cloth is an evenly-woven fabric that creates a grid-like effect forming holes into which the stitches will be placed. Since this particular Aida cloth is woven so that there are 11 holes per inch, it is referred to as 11-count Aida cloth.

THE NEEDLE

The needle is blunt-tipped since your stitches will be placed in the holes in the fabric and you will not need to pierce the cloth. This type of needle is called a Tapestry Needle. For most cross-stitch, a Size 24 Tapestry Needle is recommended.

THE THREAD

The thread used for cross-stitching is DMC Six Strand Embroidery Floss, the highest quality Floss available. If you look at the cut end of the Floss, you can clearly see the 6 separate strands which are gently twisted to create the Floss. To cross-stitch on 11-count Aida cloth, you will work with only 3 of the 6 strands.

Thread your needle with three strands of Dark Green Floss (DMC color number 561).

Find the center of the charted design (black square).

Now find the center of the Aida cloth by folding it first lengthwise and then across the width. The point at which the folds meet is the center.

From the center of the fabric, count 13 squares toward the top and 3 squares to the left. You will begin to embroider the top of the wreath. From the back of the fabric, bring the needle up through hole A (*See Fig. 1*). Next, place the needle down through hole B. Skip one space and bring the needle up through hole C, and down through hole D. Skip three more spaces and make two more half crosses (from E to F and G to H).

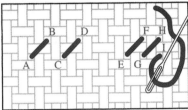

Now you may complete the cross-stitches (*See Fig. 2*). From the back, bring your needle up at I and then down again at F; up at G and down at J; up at K and down at L; up at M and down at N. You have now completed the first row! Now drop down one row, count the number of stitches, and begin your next row at O.

Follow the chart carefully as to the placement and the colors of the stitches. Complete each row as described above, placing the stitches across then crossing back over them.

When you get to the sections of the wreath which are divided, work each side section separately; don't cross over the center area.

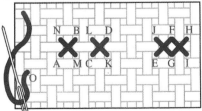

Make sure all of your cross stitches are made in the same direction so that the effect will be even.

Embroidered Christmas-tree ornament.

(DMC Corporation)

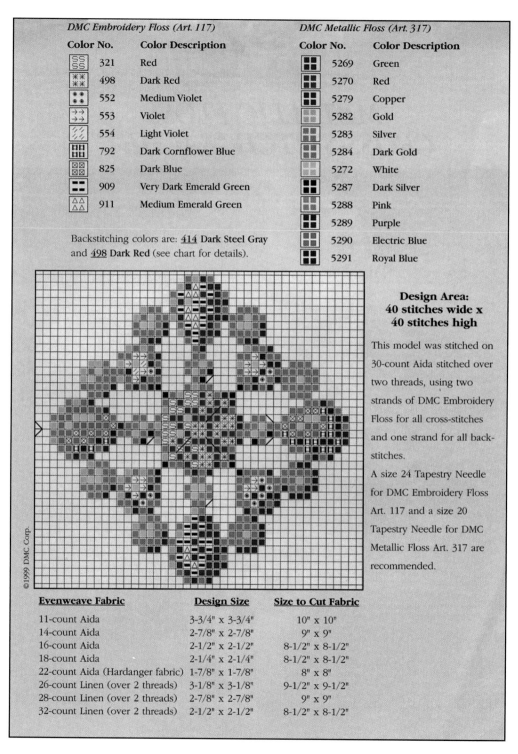

DMC Embroidery Floss (Art. 117)

	Color No.	Color Description
	321	Red
	498	Dark Red
	552	Medium Violet
	553	Violet
	554	Light Violet
	792	Dark Cornflower Blue
	825	Dark Blue
	909	Very Dark Emerald Green
	911	Medium Emerald Green

Backstitching colors are: <u>414</u> **Dark Steel Gray** and <u>498</u> **Dark Red** (see chart for details).

DMC Metallic Floss (Art. 317)

	Color No.	Color Description
	5269	Green
	5270	Red
	5279	Copper
	5282	Gold
	5283	Silver
	5284	Dark Gold
	5272	White
	5287	Dark Silver
	5288	Pink
	5289	Purple
	5290	Electric Blue
	5291	Royal Blue

**Design Area:
40 stitches wide x
40 stitches high**

This model was stitched on 30-count Aida stitched over two threads, using two strands of DMC Embroidery Floss for all cross-stitches and one strand for all back-stitches.

A size 24 Tapestry Needle for DMC Embroidery Floss Art. 117 and a size 20 Tapestry Needle for DMC Metallic Floss Art. 317 are recommended.

©1999 DMC Corp.

Evenweave Fabric	Design Size	Size to Cut Fabric
11-count Aida	3-3/4" x 3-3/4"	10" x 10"
14-count Aida	2-7/8" x 2-7/8"	9" x 9"
16-count Aida	2-1/2" x 2-1/2"	8-1/2" x 8-1/2"
18-count Aida	2-1/4" x 2-1/4"	8-1/2" x 8-1/2"
22-count Aida (Hardanger fabric)	1-7/8" x 1-7/8"	8" x 8"
26-count Linen (over 2 threads)	3-1/8" x 3-1/8"	9-1/2" x 9-1/2"
28-count Linen (over 2 threads)	2-7/8" x 2-7/8"	9" x 9"
32-count Linen (over 2 threads)	2-1/2" x 2-1/2"	8-1/2" x 8-1/2"

Embroidered Mosaic pattern for linens or a pillow.

(DMC Corporation)

Floral Design Diagrams

DMC Color No.		Description
334	← →	Blue
743	← →	Yellow
3347	← →	Green
3348	← →	Light Green

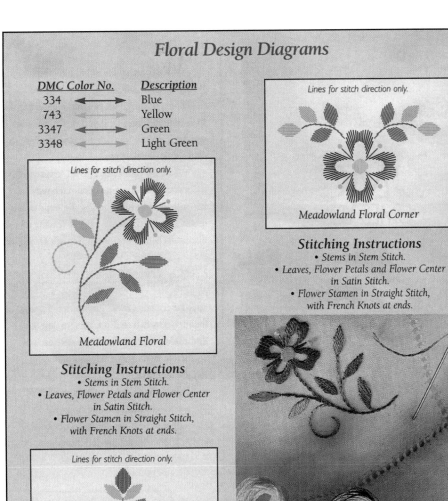

Lines for stitch direction only.

Meadowland Floral Corner

Stitching Instructions
- Stems in Stem Stitch.
- Leaves, Flower Petals and Flower Center in Satin Stitch.
- Flower Stamen in Straight Stitch, with French Knots at ends.

Lines for stitch direction only.

Meadowland Floral

Stitching Instructions
- Stems in Stem Stitch.
- Leaves, Flower Petals and Flower Center in Satin Stitch.
- Flower Stamen in Straight Stitch, with French Knots at ends.

Lines for stitch direction only.

Meadowland Floral Bud

Stitching Instructions
- Stems in Stem Stitch.
- Leaves and Flowers in Satin Stitch.
- French Knots placed as shown in diagram.

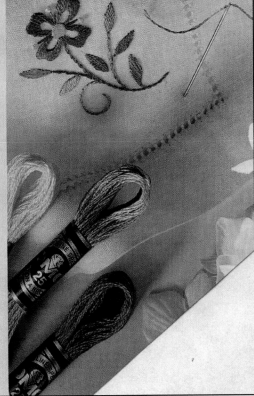

Floral designs to transfer and embroider on napkins.

(DMC Corporation)

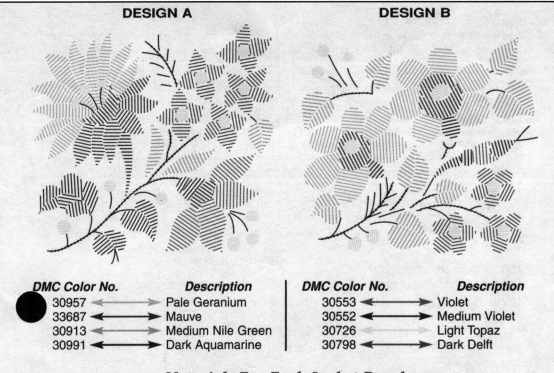

DESIGN A		**DESIGN B**	
DMC Color No.	**Description**	**DMC Color No.**	**Description**
30957 ← →	Pale Geranium	30553 ← →	Violet
33687 ← →	Mauve	30552 ← →	Medium Violet
30913 ← →	Medium Nile Green	30726 ← →	Light Topaz
30991 ← →	Dark Aquamarine	30798 ← →	Dark Delft

Materials For Each Sachet Pouch

- One skein each of DMC Rayon Floss (Art. No. 1008): No. 30552, Medium Violet; No. 30553, Violet; No. 30726, Light Topaz; No. 30798, Dark Delft; No. 30913, Medium Nile Green; No. 30957, Pale Geranium; No. 30991, Dark Aquamarine; No. 33687, Mauve
- Iron-on transfer of your choice
- Two 7-inch square pieces of ecru 28-count evenweave linen
- Size 24 tapestry needle
- Small, circular embroidery hoop
- Small, sharp scissors
- DMC Cebelia Crochet Cotton, (Article

167G) size 10, ecru and size 5 steel crochet hook (optional)
OR
One yard 1/4-inch wide ecru lace trim, one yard and matching sewing thread and needle (optional)
- Double-sided 1/4-inch wide, ecru satin ribbon
- Polyester fiberfill
- Potpourri, scent of your choice
- Miscellaneous items: iron; sewing machine; matching sewing threads; straight pins; thick terry cloth towel

Pretty patterns to transfer, embroider, and make into sachets.

(DMC Corporation)

Stitching Instructions

1. Use two 12-inch strands of Rayon Floss for all stitching.
2. Following the stitch illustrations, stitch the design using the following stitches:
   - Satin stitch all leaves, flower petals, buds and circles following Color and Symbol Key.
   - Stem stitch all long, primary stems using No. 30913 Medium Nile Green Rayon Floss.
   - Straight stitch all short, secondary stems using 30991 Dark Aquamarine Rayon Floss.
3. When beginning the Stem and Straight Stitches, leave a one-inch tail of Rayon Floss on the back of the fabric. Holding the Rayon Floss tail in place with your finger, make your first few stitches, catching the tail and anchoring it under them.

   When beginning the Satin Stitch, make a few small stitches within the area to be stitched. These stitches will be covered when you work the Satin Stitch.

   To end your stitching, run the needle under a couple of stitches on the back, leaving a small loop. Pass the needle through the loop and gently pull to make a tiny knot. Run the needle under several stitches, then trim the Rayon Floss.
4. Stitch the design following the Color Key and the Stitch Direction Lines on page 2. Work all the Satin Stitches first and then the Stem Stitches. Work the Straight Stitches last.

Finishing Instructions

1. Place the stitched design face down on a thick terry cloth towel and press to remove any wrinkles.
2. Pin the stitched square and the second square of linen right sides together. Using a 1/4-inch seam allowance machine stitch around them, leaving a 3 to 4 inch opening on the bottom side. Turn the pouch right side out, gently poking out the corners.
3. Fill the sachet pouch with a combination of fiberfill and potpourri.
4. Slip stitch the bottom opening closed.
5. To trim the sachet pouch, you may either crochet your favorite edging pattern using DMC Cebelia (Article 167G), size 10, ecru crochet thread or purchase a 1/4-inch wide lace trim.
6. If using your favorite crochet edging pattern, start by working a row of evenly-spaced single crochet stitches around the edges of the sachet pouch. Note: Work three single crochet stitches in each corner.
7. If using a purchased lace trim, slip stitch it around the edges of the sachet pouch.
8. To add an optional hanging loop, fold a 3- to 4-inch piece of the crocheted or purchased lace trim in half and stitch it to the back of the upper right-hand corner of the sachet.

(DMC Corporation)

(DMC Corporation)

HEART

This **Heart** model was stitched on 18-count Aida using two strands of DMC Embroidery Floss for all Cross-stitches and one strand for all Backstitch. A Size 26 Tapestry Needle is recommended.

DESIGN AREA:
25 stitches high x 95 stitches wide

EVENWEAVE FABRIC	DESIGN SIZE	SIZE TO CUT FABRIC
11-count Aida	2³/₈" x 8³/₄"	8¹/₂" x 15"
14-count Aida	1⁷/₈" x 7"	8" x 13"
16-count Aida	1⁵/₈" x 6"	8" x 12"
18-count Aida	1¹/₂" x 5³/₈"	7¹/₂" x 11¹/₂"
22-count Aida (Hardanger Fabric)	1¹/₄" x 4³/₈"	7¹/₂" x 10¹/₂"
26-count Linen (over 2 threads)	2" x 7³/₈"	8" x 13¹/₂"
28-count Linen (over 2 threads)	1⁷/₈" x 7"	8" x 13"
32-count Linen (over 2 threads)	1⁵/₈" x 6"	8¹/₂" x 12"

OTHER STITCHING INSTRUCTIONS:

USE **ONE** STRAND TO WORK ALL *BACKSTITCHES* IN THE FOLLOWING COLORS:

3837 - Grape colored flowers
3842 - Turquoise and Lavender Blue colored flowers
3847 - Leaves
3857 - Raspberry colored flowers and branches

These finished pieces are only suggestions for use with these **Collector's Edition** designs. Use your imagination to finish your cross-stitch piece in the method of your choice.

DMC No.	Color Description	DMC No.	Color Description	DMC No.	Color Description	DMC No.	Color Description
A 3831	Dark Raspberry	J 3840	Light Lavender Blue	S 3849	Light Teal Green	& 3858	Medium Rosewood
B 3832	Medium Raspberry	K 3841	Pale Baby Blue	T 3850	Dark Bright Green	2 3859	Light Rosewood
C 3833	Light Raspberry	L 3842	Dark Wedgwood	U 3851	Light Bright Green	3 3860	Cocoa
D 3834	Dark Grape	M 3843	Electric Blue	V 3852	Very Dark Straw	4 3861	Light Cocoa
E 3835	Medium Grape	N 3844	Dark Bright Turquoise	W 3853	Dark Autumn Gold	5 3862	Dark Mocha Beige
F 3836	Light Grape	O 3845	Medium Bright Turquoise	X 3854	Medium Autumn Gold	6 3863	Medium Mocha Beige
G 3837	Ultra Dark Lavender	P 3846	Light Bright Turquoise	Y 3855	Light Autumn Gold	7 3864	Light Mocha Beige
H 3838	Dark Lavender Blue	Q 3847	Dark Teal Green	Z 3856	Ultra Very Light Mahogany	8 3865	Winter White
I 3839	Medium Lavender Blue	R 3848	Medium Teal Green	? 3857	Dark Rosewood	9 3866	Ultra Very Light Mocha Brown

A heart motif to cross stitch on clothing or linens.

(DMC Corporation)

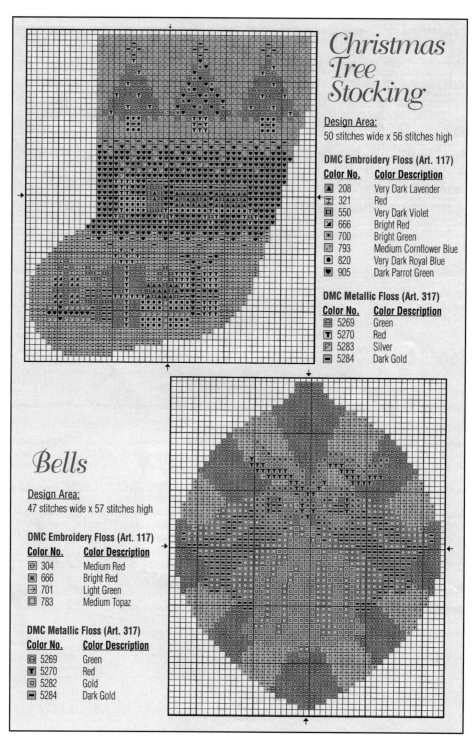

Christmas Tree Stocking

Design Area:
50 stitches wide x 56 stitches high

DMC Embroidery Floss (Art. 117)

Color No.	Color Description
▲ 208	Very Dark Lavender
⊤ 321	Red
⊞ 550	Very Dark Violet
⊠ 666	Bright Red
✳ 700	Bright Green
∴ 793	Medium Cornflower Blue
● 820	Very Dark Royal Blue
▼ 905	Dark Parrot Green

DMC Metallic Floss (Art. 317)

Color No.	Color Description
⊡ 5269	Green
⊤ 5270	Red
⊘ 5283	Silver
▬ 5284	Dark Gold

Bells

Design Area:
47 stitches wide x 57 stitches high

DMC Embroidery Floss (Art. 117)

Color No.	Color Description
⊙ 304	Medium Red
✳ 666	Bright Red
→ 701	Light Green
☐ 783	Medium Topaz

DMC Metallic Floss (Art. 317)

Color No.	Color Description
⊡ 5269	Green
⊤ 5270	Red
⊡ 5282	Gold
▬ 5284	Dark Gold

A Christmas-tree stocking, bell, and floral arrow (next page) ornaments to needlepoint.
(DMC Corporation)

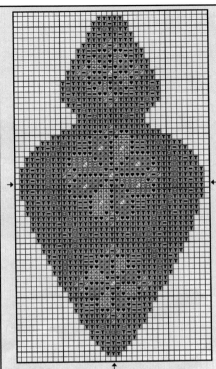

Floral Arrow

<u>Design Area:</u> 35 stitches wide x 63 stitches high

DMC Embroidery Floss (Art. 117)

Color No.		Color Description
◩	White	White
⊞	321	Red
⊠	666	Bright Red
▼	820	Very Dark Royal Blue
✳	905	Dark Parrot Green

DMC Metallic Floss (Art. 317)

Color No.		Color Description
◎	5269	Green
⊤	5270	Red
☑	5283	Silver
▬	5284	Dark Gold

Continental Stitch Continued...

At end of each row, finish last stitch, then turn the canvas completely around and start new row in line with row just completed.

Finishing Instructions

1. Apply low-loft iron-on interfacing, slightly smaller than ornament, on back. Add self-adhesive felt same size as ornament.

2. For cording, you will be making three cords, to be combined later. To make first cord, select three colors of DMC Metallic or Cotton Floss (you can mix them). Cut each color twice the length around ornament. Knot three colors together at both ends.

3. Close top knot in a drawer to hold it. Twist the DMC Floss clockwise until tight. Maintaining tension, tape ends to a work surface. Make two more cords the same length.

4. Keeping tension, place top knot of all three cords into a drawer and close. Grasp bottom knots and twist them together counter-clockwise until cord shortens. Maintaining tension, tape new twisted cord below knots.

5. Slip one end of twisted cord under felt backing and cut away tape. Slip stitch cord to ornament. Tuck end of cord under felt.

6. Repeat same three-cord method with Green Metallic and Cotton Floss to make ornament hanger.

Working With Plastic Canvas

• Each line on the chart represents one bar of plastic canvas. When counting on plastic canvas, count the bars, NOT the holes. When cutting plastic canvas, cut in the space between two bars.
• Before cutting shape, lightly mark its outline on the plastic canvas with a washable, felt-tip pen. Using household scissors, cut out shape. Trim off the plastic nubs. Clean off the marker outlines.
• Use the Continental Stitch to stitch ornament, using short lengths (approx. 12") of Metallic Floss. When design is completed, overcast the canvas edges.

Continental Stitch

Working horizontally, start at upper right and work each row of stitches from right to left. Form each stitch by bringing needle up at 1, down at 2, up at 3, down at 4, etc.

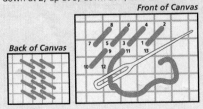

Front of Canvas

Back of Canvas

Designs by Catherine Reurs

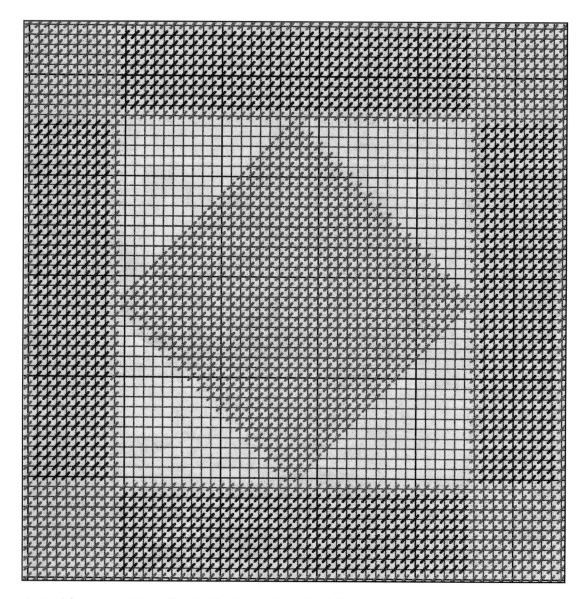

An Amish ornament to needlepoint (see instructions that follow).

Amish Diamond
Materials
14 meshclear or plastic canvas, 6 x 6 inches
1 spool each Kreinik #16 (medium) braid in red 003V (thinest lines),
emerald 009HL (outline sympbols), pearl 032 (blank spaces), and Aztec Gold
202HL (thick lines)(or similar colors))
1 #22 tapestry needle

Begin by stitching the entire outline in the gold, using asingle strand of
the metallic thread.

Cut an 18 inch length of metallic.

Thread your needle and begin to stitch the entire outline in gold.

All the stitches in the piece are needlepoint tent stitches, slanting over
a single intersection from lower left to upper right.

Now stitch the green areas, then the red. Most of the piece is now filled in.

Finally end by stitching the remaining areas in cream metallic using the
same stitch.

To finish the ornament. Cut the plastic canvas just outside the stitched
area. Now cut another piece of plastic canvas the same size.

Cut a piece of green metallic about 12 inches long and tie the two ends
together. This will become your hanger for the ornament.

Put the tie between the two pieces of canvas and let it hang out one corner.

Using the green metallic you will sew the two pieces of canvas together.
Begin by running your thread through several stitches on the reverse of the
stitched side. Make sure the hanger is hanging out and start sewing the
two sides together, beginning at the corner by the hanger.

To do this you will come out one hole ,go over the edge of the canvas and go
back in (on the same side of the ornament) in the very next hole. This is
called overcasting and is an excellent way to finish plastic canvas pieces.

Work all the way around the ornament and then tie off the thread and tuck
the ends into the corner where the hanger comes out.

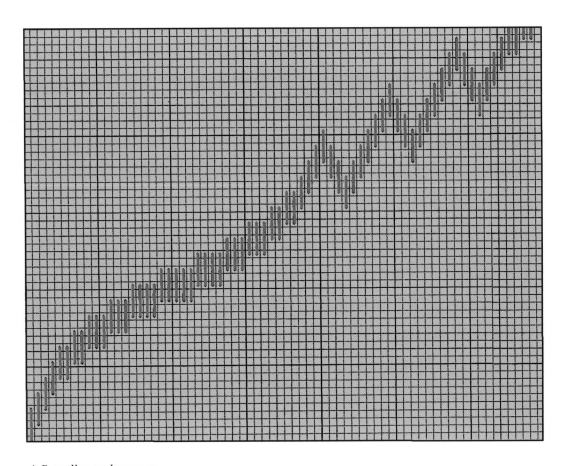

A Bargello eyeglass case.

(© 2000 by Janet M. Perry [needlepoint.about.com], licensed to About, Inc. Used by permission of About, Inc., which can be found on the Web at www.About.com. All rights reserved.)

Bargello eyeglass case

2 pieces 18 mesh mono or interlock canvas, 6 x 8 inches
1 skein each Brown Paper PAckages Silk & Ivory in 04 peach, 21 terra cotta,
37 rhubarb and 14 burgundy
8″ of soft lining fabric
Sewing thread to match lining
Hand-sewing needle

2 pieces 18 mesh mono or interlock canvas, 6 x 8 inches
1 skein each Brown Paper PAckages Silk & Ivory in 04 peach, 21 terra cotta,
37 rhubarb and 14 burgundy

Bargello charts typically show only one line of the pattern, which you stitch first to establish the pattern. Begin by marking a rectangle on your canvas about 5-6 inches long and 3-4 inches wide, depending on the size of your glasses. Three by five is generally large enough for most glasses.

Begin stitching in the lower left corner using the Brugundy thread. Stitch one entire line. If your rectangle is wider than the chart, just repeat the pattern from where it leaves off.

Stitch row by row, follwing this order of colors: burgundy, rhubarb, terra cotta, peach, burgundy and so on.

Finishing the case

Trim each edge of canvas to ½ inch. Turn back top edge along tent stitches; turn back the other three edges along the canvas thread next to the Bargello stitches. Miter corners (see right). With wrong sides of needlepoint together, fold case along vertical center; match threads along bottom and side edges. Sew together with whipstitches, first across bottom, then along side of the eyeglass case. Reinforce the top corner by forming three whipstitches in the same hole, fanning them around the corner.

Cut lining piece 8½ inches wide by 8 inches long. With right sides together, fold lining in half along vertical center. Form a ⅝-inch seam; trim. Turn top edge back ⅜ inch. Slip lining into case; align seams of lining and case. Stitch lining to case along top edge.

Excess canvas at the edges is trimmed to ½″ before turning. Turn top edge along the needle other three along thread next to the stitches. **To miter corners,** trim canvas diagonally acr (A); fold back across corner (B); turn back edges on each side of corner and tack (C).

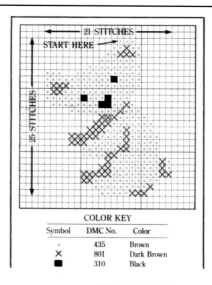

COLOR KEY

Symbol	DMC No.	Color
°	435	Brown
×	801	Dark Brown
■	310	Black

THE MATERIALS

THE CLOTH

Aida cloth is an evenly-woven fabric that creates a grid-like effect forming holes into which the stitches will be placed. Since this particular Aida cloth is woven so that there are 11 holes per inch, it is referred to as 11-count Aida cloth.

THE NEEDLE

The needle is blunt-tipped since your stitches will be placed in the holes in the fabric and you will not need to pierce the cloth. This type of needle is called a Tapestry Needle. For most cross-stitch, a Size 24 Tapestry Needle is recommended.

THE THREAD

The thread used for cross-stitching is DMC Six Strand Embroidery Floss, the highest quality Floss available. If you look at the cut end of the Floss, you can clearly see the 6 separate strands which are gently twisted to create the Floss. To cross-stitch on 11-count Aida cloth, you will work with only 3 of the 6 strands.

Thread your needle with three strands of Brown Floss (DMC color number 435).

Find the center of the charted design (circled).

Now find the center of the Aida cloth by folding it first lengthwise and then across the width. The point at which the folds meet is the center.

From the center of the fabric, count 12 squares toward the top and 2 squares to the right. You will begin to embroider the bear's ear. From the back of the fabric, bring the needle up through hole A (See Fig. 1). Next, place the needle down through hole B. Now bring the needle up through hole C, and down through hole D. Make one more half cross (from E to F).

Fig. 1

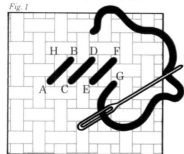

Now, you may complete the cross stitches (See Fig. 2). From the back, bring your needle up at G and then down again at D; up at E and down at B; up at C and down at H. You have now completed the first row! Now drop down one row, count the number of stitches, and begin your next row at I.

Follow the chart carefully as to the placement and the colors of the stitches.

Complete each row as described above, placing the stitches across then crossing back over them.

A darling teddy bear to cross stitch.

(DMC Corporation)

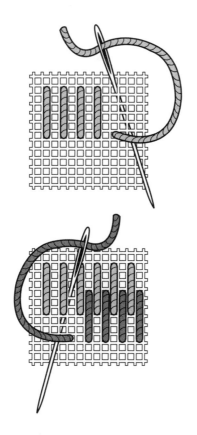

The Gobelin filling stitch produces a basketweave effect.

For the next and succeeding rows, work the stitches between the stitches of the previous row. The base of each row should be three horizontal threads below the base of the previous stitches.

Random Long Stitch

Work the *random long* stitch the same as the upright Gobelin stitch, but vary the length of the stitches by working them randomly over 1, 2, 3, or 4 horizontal threads. Use this stitch to quickly fill in large areas.

Long and Short Stitch

The *long and short* stitch combines one row of long stitches with two rows of shorter stitches. It is quick and easy to work. Make four stitches, moving up one canvas thread for each stitch and covering four horizontal threads with each stitch. Now work three stitches, moving down *to the right* one thread for each. Continue the same steps and a zigzag will begin to form.

*The random long stitch
quickly fills large areas.*

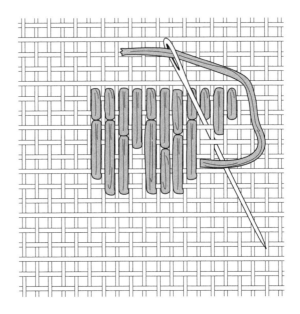

*The long and short stitch
creates a tweedlike effect.*

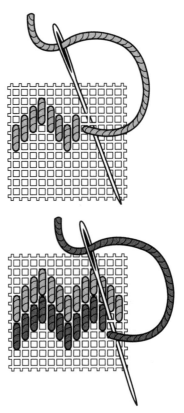

Work the next two rows in the same manner, but take smaller stitches worked over two threads. Continue working one row of the long stitches alternating with two rows of the short stitches.

Star

Star stitches are composite stitches made from straight, diagonal, and crossed stitches. They are large stitches that form starlike shapes. They can be framed with other stitches emphasizing a geometric shape. Be sure to use a mono canvas and thick yarn so that the mesh is covered. A very popular star stitch is the large Algerian eye stitch.

Large Algerian Eye Stitch

For the *large Algerian eye* stitch, you must first form a large square "star." To do this, work 16 stitches clockwise from the same hole, taking your yarn over four canvas threads or canvas intersections at the corners of the square star that is formed, leaving two canvas threads unworked between each stitch at the outer part of the stitches.

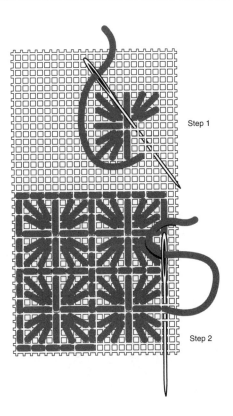

Step 1

Step 2

The large algerian eye stitch resembles little boxes with starlike patterns.

Frame your square stars with backstitches that are worked over two canvas threads.

143

Looped

Looped stitches are knotted loops that add unusual texture to a canvas. Some looped stitches can be cut to form a shaggy *pile* like a rug. Others remain loopy.

Needlework 101

Pile is a furry surface formed on fabrics by short raised loops of yarn that are sometimes sheared.

Velvet Stitch

The *velvet* stitch is made in the same way that velvet fabric is woven. Its loops are cut to create a pile. Just like velvet. Work this stitch on double, or Penelope, canvas or any rug canvas.

Bring the needle through to the front of the canvas at the bottom left corner and, by working left to right, take a diagonal backstitch over two canvas intersections up to the right.

Bring the needle up to the right again, and insert it in the same place where the needle first came up to start the backstitch. Hold down the thread with your finger and make a loop; take the needle down to the right at the top of the backstitch. Bring the needle out two horizontal threads down.

The velvet stitch is worked in loops that are cut to form a pile.

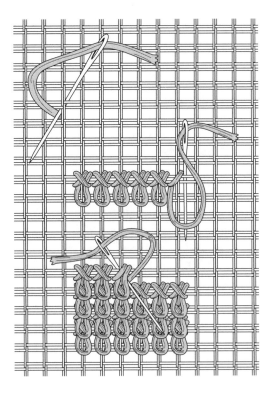

Continue to hold down the loop with your finger while you take a diagonal backstitch up to the left and over two canvas intersections.

Repeat these steps to the end of the row. For the next row and the ones to follow, keep stitching above the previous row. When you have completed your work, cut the loops to form a pile and trim to desired length.

A Stitch in Time

When you form loops, slip a knitting needle (or crotchet hook, pencil, etc.) into the loop to size it. This will help you create more uniform loops.

The Least You Need to Know

➤ Tent stitches are small diagonal stitches that are worked in the same direction over one intersection of canvas.

➤ Diagonal stitches are worked so that they are stitched in a slanted direction over the canvas threads.

➤ Crossed stitches are formed by either diagonal or straight stitches crossing over each other.

➤ Straight stitches are easy and quickly stitched. They can be interesting if different lengths are combined.

➤ Star stitches are composite stitches made from straight, diagonal, and crossed stitches.

➤ Looped stitches are knotted loops that add unusual texture to a canvas.

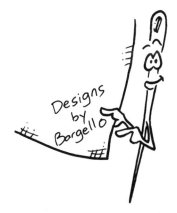

Designs by Bargello

Bargello Design

Bargello design is a very popular traditional needlepoint work, often referred to as "flamestitch" or "Florentine." Its stitches are straight, graduating, and upright, forming zigzag patterned rows. By changing the size and spacing of the stitches, the zigzags can be smoothed into curves or sharpened into peaks. Whether you're looking to recreate a good old Charlie Brown zigzag look or a more advanced fish scale motif, this is an excellent technique to use.

Bargello is best used for patterned design work. In other words, you won't be creating people's faces or Smiley, your pet parakeet, with this technique. But you can create wonderful texture and original designs by combining stitches and using different colors of yarn.

Bargello work has become a popular choice because it covers mono (single) canvas quite easily and quickly and can be worked in very colorful rows. Take a stab at Bargello and see what the fuss is all about!

Effects of Color

All Bargello work is stitched in rows of different colors. A three-color pattern, using colors from the same family, forms a *monochromatic* tone. For example, pale blue, medium blue, and dark blue will create a calm, soft look. Using three very different colors such as red, green, and blue will have quite the opposite effect—bolder, more jarring to the eye, and a more distinctive pattern.

Use the color wheel in this book to inspire color combinations. Combining *harmonious* colors (colors that are next to each other on the color wheel) is another method. A combination of blue, blue-violet, and violet illustrates a harmony of colors.

You can even use primary colors for wonderful possibilities. If the intensity of the pure hues is too strong for you, substitute gold for yellow, claret for red, and navy for blue. The primaries will take on a whole new feeling! Another triangle of colors, the secondaries of violet, orange, and green, might work for you as well.

As you know from Chapter 2, "Well-Designed Needle Art," *complementary* colors are pairings that are opposite each other on the color wheel, such as red/green, orange/blue, and yellow-green/red-violet. For a nice three-color combination, try adding a lighter shade of one of the two complementary colors.

For more color inspirations, look at what others have chosen for their color schemes, whether from prepackaged kits or from designer canvases in your local specialty needlepoint shop.

Bargello Basics

Bargello patterns are worked horizontally across the canvas. In order to get nice, even rows and to achieve the zigzag design, you'll need to create a guideline.

Since the first line of stitching is worked from the center of the canvas out to both the left and right edges, create your guideline at the center. Find the center point by dividing your canvas into quarters with a felt-tip marker. This forms the beginning of your design. Work your rows from left to right and right to left, above and below the center point, until your canvas is filled.

Clever Crafter

Florentine work is thought to have been brought to Florence from Hungary in the fifteenth century by a Hungarian girl who married a Medici prince.

Bargello stitches are sometimes quite long, so the tail of the thread must be firmly secured. A backstitch can firmly hold the beginning or ending threads.

Fundamental Zigzag

The *zigzag* stitch is the easiest one to learn and is the basis for all types of Bargello stitches. Start with a "4–2" zigzag pattern, which means that the stitch length is four horizontal threads, and that the step up, or down, for the next stitch is two horizontal threads.

To begin, bring your needle out at the center point (where the felt-tip marker lines on your canvas intersect). Take your needle up four horizontal threads, and insert it to the back of the canvas. Then, to make the *step,* bring out the needle two horizontal threads below the top of the last stitch and one vertical thread to the right.

Repeat those first steps three times going *up* the canvas. On the third stitch, bring your needle out six horizontal threads below the top of your last stitch.

Needlework 101

Step is the term for the number of crosswise canvas threads between the bases of neighboring stitches.

The easiest way to learn Bargello is to start with the basic zigzag.

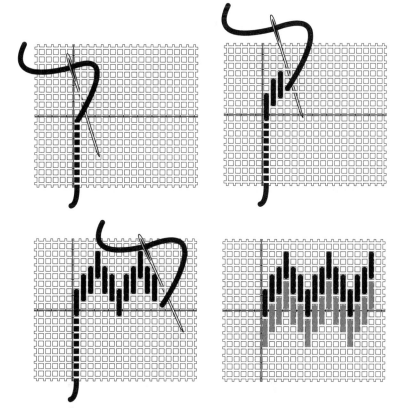

Work the next three stitches *down* the canvas to form the first upside-down V of the zigzag pattern. Repeat all these steps, alternating three stitches up and three stitches down the canvas.

Work your next color into the base of the first zigzag row.

A Stitch in Time

You can use a 22-inch-long working thread in Bargello work because the thread slides through the canvas easily.

Adding Curves

The basic zigzag can be adjusted to form a curvy pattern.

At the top and base of each zigzag peak, work two or more stitches the same length as the preceding stitch.

More than two stitches will create an elongated curve, and just two stitches will create a more peaked curve.

Practice a few continuous curves before starting a large Bargello project. They are easy to master but require thinking!

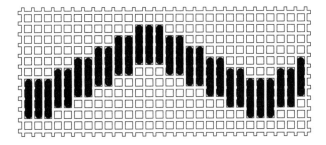

Catching Waves

To create a *wavy Bargello* pattern, apply the curvy technique, but elongate the curves by adding more stitches at the zigzag peak.

In Bargello, the more stitches used to form the peak, the longer the wave.

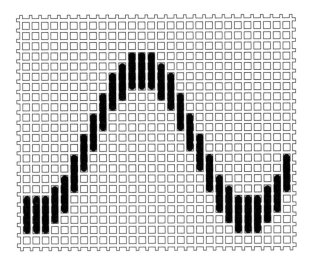

The wave technique is different from creating curves because you are adding stitches at the end of your zigzags and not piling them above the peaks.

Fish Scales

For a fish scale–looking row, use the same method as you did for the curves but, at the base, leave only one stitch to form a peak. This will form the scales. Use this to form a somewhat soft scalloped pattern for a change from hard peaks in the zigzag patterns.

A Stitch in Time

Since you change colors often in Bargello work, save yourself some time by having several needles threaded with the different colors that you are using. You won't have to keep rethreading.

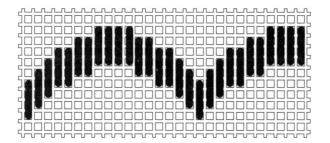

Keep the tops of the peaks curvy and the bases pointed to form a Bargello scalloped effect, like that of fish scales.

Two-Way Bargello

In *two-way Bargello*, the pattern is reversed in the second row to form a mirror image.

The first row that you stitch is the beginning of the pattern. Work the first row like the basic zigzag stitch shown in the first section of this chapter. Turn your canvas upside down, and then stitch another row of basic zigzags to form a mirror image of the first row.

Since the second row will be created in reverse, you will have empty spaces in between the two rows. Fill the empty spots with upright stitches in a different color of yarn. Using upright stitches will offset the look of the two-way Bargello pattern so that you don't lose the effect you were going for in the first place!

A Stitch in Time

Attractive and contrasting patterns can be achieved by combining curves and steep peaks. Vary the shades of your yarn colors to add the illusion of depth to your pattern.

151

To form the mirror image of two-way Bargello, the bases of the rows must meet.

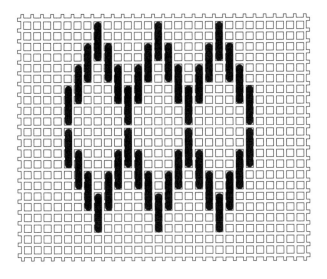

Four-Way Bargello

The *four-way Bargello* stitch is perfect for square designs like bags or pillows. As in all Bargello, the central stitch starts the pattern and continues out to the edges. When you do this in four-way Bargello, you'll form one large motif.

Cut your canvas into a square. Mark two diagonal lines; go from corner to corner with a felt-tip marker. Make four stitches in the center like a cross, as shown in the following figure.

Continue the pattern in this manner, stitching each quarter of the canvas in an identical way, as shown in the following figure.

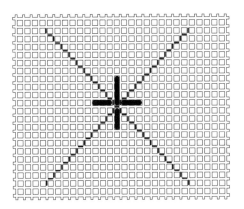
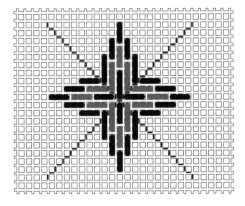

The four-way Bargello forms a unique pattern that is perfect for a pillow or bag design.

Charting Your Own Designs

Now that you have learned some of the basic stitches, you can think about charting your own patterns and colors. The possible stitch combinations are endless!

Get out your graph paper, and fill in the squares to correspond to a square of your canvas. Use a ruler to keep your newly charted lines straight and your pattern easy to follow. Your linear markings will represent the stitches to make the pattern. Use different colors to represent the colors that you will use.

Clever Crafter

Hold a mirror up to your new design. The reverse image will help you to see a new pattern to repeat.

Be sure to always start at the center of the design and work out toward the edges. This helps to keep your pattern visually balanced.

The Least You Need to Know

➤ Bargello design is a very popular traditional needlepoint technique often referred to as "flamestitch" or "Florentine" work.

➤ Bargello patterns are worked horizontally across the canvas.

➤ The basic zigzag is the easiest Bargello stitch to learn.

➤ All Bargello work is stitched in rows of different colors.

➤ Use the color wheel to inspire color combinations.

Part 5

Advanced Needlepoint

Now you're really making the grade! Get ready to learn some special effects, how to design your own needlepoint, and ways to finish off a project. You'll learn freehand needlepoint and different effects that will add flair to your work. At the end of this section, consider yourself a full-fledged needlecrafter!

Chapter 15

Designing Your Own Needlepoint

In This Chapter

➤ Finding inspirations for needlepoint

➤ Creating different types of samplers

➤ Trying your hand at freehand design

➤ Transferring large designs onto canvas sections

Designing your own needlepoint is so much fun because there are so many subjects, stitches, colors, and techniques to choose from. Check your files (if you haven't collected any project ideas, now is the time to start!), and brush up on the transferring designs you learned in Chapter 12, "Needlepoint Tips and Tricks."

Adding a twist to borrowed ideas or creating your own designs is the most rewarding part of needlepoint. Embellish plain designs with decorative stitches or interesting colors of yarn. You can use part of a larger design on a very small piece, thus creating quite a dramatic effect. Or, go all out and create your own patterns from scratch! An original design will show off your personal style.

Lettering and signing your pieces also add that something extra; something that says, "I made this." And what could be more unique than the combination of an original design and an item that is handmade? It will become a priceless gift for someone special, or an item you will cherish for a long time.

Inspirations for Needlepoint Ideas

Designing your own needlepoint allows you to stitch your favorite subjects, like your children, your home, your pet turtle Sparky, or anything else that is special to you. Still having trouble deciding on something? What about re-creating a favorite picture? How about stitching some letters or a personal message on canvas?

Items in your home, like bouquets of flowers, china patterns, and wall-covering designs, provide ideas for colors and shapes to sketch. Once you start noticing patterns in everything, there will be no stopping you! If you really get into borrowing designs for needlepoint from everything you see, it's a good idea to carry a small sketchbook wherever you go. You could spot a beautiful embroidered purse while on a train and only have a tissue to sketch on. The tissue will work fine as a makeshift sketch pad as long as you don't have a cold!

The many items that you can needlepoint. Some projects to consider for your designs include:

➤ Pillows

➤ Picture frames

➤ Brick covers for doorstops

➤ Gift boxes

➤ Handbags

➤ Slippers

➤ Bookmarks

➤ Holiday ornaments

➤ Holiday cards

➤ Dollhouse rugs

➤ Bell pulls

➤ Footstool covers

➤ Chair covers

➤ Samplers

These ideas are just the beginning of how you can use needlepoint to convey your personal style.

Decorator's Do's and Don'ts

Don't forget to save room! Always allow a border of at least three inches on each side when planning your design. You will need this extra material to stretch the canvas.

Clever Crafter

When I took needlework classes in Belgium, I chose a sampler as my project. I fashioned a grid pattern that alternated various stitches with pictorials of places that I had visited. I stitched my name and dates to give the sampler even more meaning. I chose Belgian colors of loden green, red, and yellow. You can do the same with a place that has meaning to you.

Sampling Samplers

As in embroidery, needlepoint samplers show off different stitches. Needlepoint samplers are stitched with straight, looped, crossed, diagonal, and star stitches, or a combination. Fabulous patterns can also be achieved with just one type of stitch!

Use a variety of colors in your sampler, and it becomes a beautiful work of art. Traditionally samplers were worked to show the various types of stitches, but pictorials were done as well. A combination of different colors and various stitches can make a great design. This is where your imagination and personal style can shine with clever expression. Embellish your sampler by stitching a message or your name with the date of your work. Use classic colors and not the latest trends, which will fade in popularity and make your work look dated. A glow-in-the-dark kitten might be cute now, but you might be quite tired of it next month!

These various samplers show the different stitches that you learned in Chapter 13, "Just Point and Stitch."

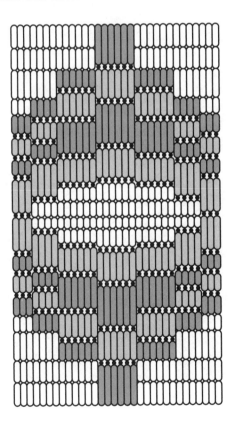

Straight stitches can make very interesting patterns.

Diagonal stitches and different colors form blocks of diagonal stripes.

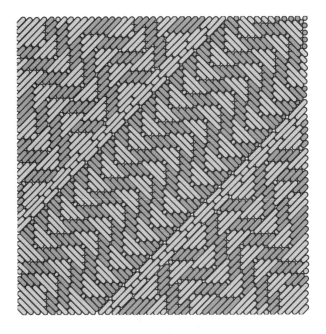

Crossed stitches and colors combine to make a diagonal motif.

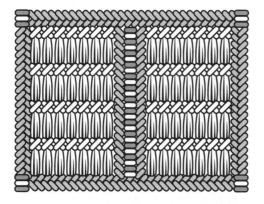

Cut loops turn into tassels on this sampler.

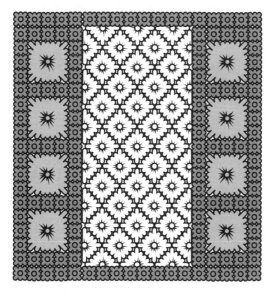

This intricate-looking sampler is composed of framed star stitches that give the effect of stars within a box.

Freehand Design

What do you do if you have a blank canvas? You could try some freehand work by drawing directly onto your canvas or stitching your own design without any guides. Both require a little courage and practice. But after you have tried a few and had successful outcomes, you'll find that stitching your own design is almost as easy as stitching a prepainted canvas. You will be making a one-of-a-kind design, and that alone is worth your effort!

Drawing Directly on Canvas

Drawing your idea on paper will give you a better sense of how the final design will look on canvas. Don't panic if drawing is not your bag—you don't need to be Monet

A Stitch in Time

If you are a little nervous about freehand painted designs, try a practice run on another blank canvas to get used to the paints and brush.

to sketch a design. Keep trying out sketches until you're happy before moving on to a canvas. Even if your first design from a sketch isn't your best work, don't give up! As in anything, the more you do it, the better you'll be.

Make sure that your sketched pattern fits the size of your canvas and the intended size of your project. You might have trouble fitting a 24-inch-tall bouquet on a 12-inch-square piece of canvas. If you are sketching a different size than your model, you will need to sketch your items to scale. For more on scale, refer to Chapter 2, "Well-Designed Needle Art."

After drawing your initial sketches, draw your design on canvas to the scale that you will stitch it in. Keep the outline of your drawing bold and distinct. Color in as much of your design as you wish with colored pencils to get an even better sense of how your design will look. After outlining and coloring in, draw vertical and horizontal lines to quarter the canvas so you can be ready to chart it on graph paper (as you learned in Chapter 12) or paint your design directly on the canvas.

Drawing or painting on canvas can be a quick and easy way to start your needlepoint design.

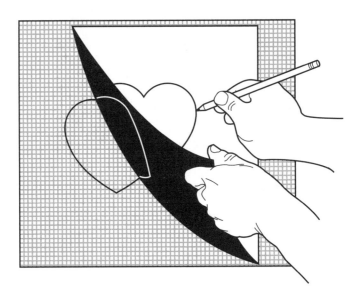

To paint on the canvas without guidelines, imagine you are creating an actual painting. Again, create clear outlines and fill in each part with paint colors that correspond to the yarn colors you will use. Acrylic paints will dry faster than thinned oil paints and will smell much better. Use white nylon brushes that are stiff so that they work well on the roughness of the canvas. Small brushes are better because large ones will cause the paints to bleed. Let the canvas dry thoroughly after painting before you pick it up again. Any movement during drying will distort the design.

Stitching Directly on Canvas

Creating a design on your canvas with stitches alone can be nerve-wracking for some and liberating for others. You'll only know which category you fit into when you try it!

Designing your own pattern on canvas allows you to be totally free in your choices of stitches and colors. Be sure to have a clear image in mind before you begin, and stitch according to that. A geometric design is easier to figure because of its up-and-down and side-to-side stitching as opposed to a very curvy design, but both can be done with ease after you get the hang of it.

Stitching freehand designs on canvas can be difficult at first, but also very rewarding!

It might be helpful to stitch some outlines or guidelines before you fill in the entire design. This will give you a better idea of how each part of the design relates in scale to the other parts. You will also be able to tell whether you like the way the design has transferred from your head onto the canvas.

After you have some stitching guidelines in place, the next step is to stitch just the outline of your design. If you are happy with that, you can fill in the rest of the design and then stitch the background. For example, if you design a motif of a flower, do the outline of the petals and the stem first. If you are satisfied with them, go ahead and fill in the petals, using different directions of stitching, and finally stitch a patterned or solid background.

Decorator's Do's and Don'ts

Don't fill in any part of your background until you've stitched all of the design! This will give you more flexibility in case you need to alter anything, because you will not have to contend with an already stitched background.

Super-Size It!

Ever wonder how large-scale designs like oversized wall tapestries or needlepoint rugs are hand-stitched? They are worked in sections, since the canvas isn't big enough to accommodate the design.

To create a large-scale design, cut your canvas into sections of equal size, remembering to leave a border for sewing the sections together once you have finished. Careful transferring of the design to the canvas is critical for a well-put-together pattern.

To section your design, first draw your pattern on paper or chart it on graph paper. Divide it into equal-sized sections that are labeled *A, B, C, D*. Cut the canvas sections, and mark the sections to correspond to the sections of the drawing. Transfer the drawings onto the canvas, and you are ready to begin. If you have drawn on graph paper, then transferring will not be necessary—you can read from the graph and begin stitching. When the work is completed, each section must be blocked and joined together (see Chapter 17, "Finishing Your Needlepoint") in the correct sequence in order to create the design you were after.

Draw your pattern on paper, and divide it into equal sections.

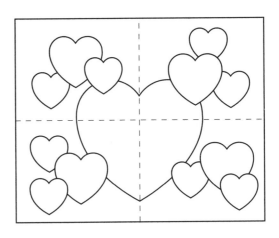

An example of transferring a large design onto canvas, along with a border allowance.

The Least You Need to Know

➤ Creating your own designs is a rewarding part of needlepoint.

➤ Samplers can show off any of the straight, diagonal, crossed, looped, or starred stitches. They can also be embellished with personal messages or initials and dates.

➤ Freehand designs can be tricky but well worth it.

➤ Large-scale designs need to be worked in sections, since your canvas may not be big enough to accommodate your design.

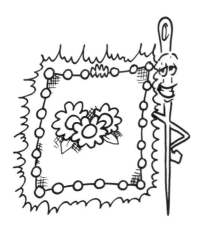

Chapter 16

Adding Your Own Flair

In This Chapter

➤ Moving backgrounds forward

➤ Getting a feel for texture

➤ Sprucing up borders

Now that you have entered the world of design, you can learn how to add pizzazz to store-bought patterns and your own needlepoint designs. Plain backgrounds can be embellished with a variety of techniques; textures can be emphasized with color, yarns, or beads; and a central motif can be framed with a stitched border.

Backgrounds

Many needlepoint designs concentrate on a central motif, like a bouquet of flowers, and pair it with a solid background. If the background is good sized, it can be a bit dull to keep stitching in the same color or in the same pattern. Keep your designs alive (and yourself awake!) by jazzing up your backgrounds. Even though you might think the background is "just the background," anything you do to spruce it up will help your overall design. There are many different ways to embellish backgrounds. Read on for only some of the endless possibilities!

Not-So-Plain Jane

"Plain" backgrounds or backgrounds of the same color can be enhanced by changing the stitches. For most stitchers, the tent stitch or the cross stitch is the stitch of choice for backgrounds, but that doesn't have to be *your* choice. The same goes for kits. You don't have to use the stitch specified in the kit, though you do have to keep in mind the amount of yarn available in the kit for the background. Try using more-interesting stitches such as the upright Gobelin, the long and short stitch, or the Byzantine. Many other stitches discussed in Chapter 13, "Just Point and Stitch," are also good choices for breaking up a plain background. The stitches will add to the pattern but not take away any focus from the main design.

Blended Tones

Needlepoint backgrounds can be subtly changed by stitching blended shades of similar colors. The main design is still the focal point, but the background has a shaded effect. Some yarns and threads are available already shaded, which makes this technique easy. If you want blended tones in the background and you don't have pre-blended yarn, you can combine strands of different colored yarns to create different combinations.

To make your own shaded yarn, select three or four similar tones of thread or yarn.

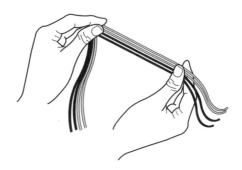

Untwist each of the different colors of yarn or threads and then recombine the different tones to make a new one.

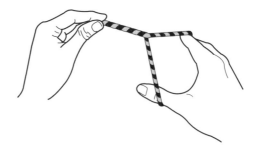

Marbled Backgrounds

Marbled effects are very beautiful, but a little more difficult to work. Try using yarn colors of very pale blues, grays, tans, and whites and a little yellow and subtle blended tones of each for different irregular horizontal patterns. Work sections in the individual colors in different sized wavy rows. This will create a subtle irregular pattern similar to that of marble.

Further enhance your work by using wool threads and highlighting areas with silk threads.

Patterned Backgrounds

Patterned backgrounds can be equally as visual as the foreground motif. They are incorporated as part of the overall design. Florals, geometrics, stripes, checks, and Bargello patterns can all be tastefully incorporated to ensure that the main motif is still the main attraction.

Try to coordinate the colors of the main motif with the background pattern for harmony in the overall design. For example, if the main motif is a sunflower in yellows, browns, and greens, needlepoint the background in a solid brown with a dot-like pattern (created from a few stitches) in yellow. Or, consider sharply contrasting the colors for a more pronounced motif.

Unworked Backgrounds

Another idea is to use fabric instead of canvas for your design. That way, you don't need to work the background—the fabric becomes the pattern.

A good fabric to use is an evenweave linen. The threads of the linen become your canvas and are distinct and easy to stitch. Also try patterned fabric—the type you can find in a sewing department for dress or curtain making. You can use the pattern lines as guidelines when you stitch.

Both linen and patterned fabric will instantly become the background design, and there is no stitching involved! By using fabric, your main needlepoint design becomes the focus, and it's a quick way to get a patterned background!

Shading Techniques

The shading technique is quite simple to do. You have to decide which method you want to use for the particular look of your needlepoint. Preshaded threads give a random shaded effect and, depending on the stitch used, you can create a shaded and textured look. For example, create a field of hay by using preshaded gold and the encroaching Gobelin stitch in rows to simulate the hay texture. The sky can be simulated by using shaded yarns in pale blues, grays, and white and a condensed Scottish stitch for texture.

Antique-looking shading is achieved by using subtle colors that you combine together yourself. These yarns produce an uneven shading, which is typical of antique or old and faded needlework pieces.

Creating Texture

To create textures with your needlepoint, use different combinations of canvas, threads/yarn, and stitching. By using just one stitch in different directions makes a pattern of texture. Combining more than one stitch will also create a textured look. If you are working with red yarn only, try working a design that includes a sampling of the stitches that we have covered. You will see how the different stitches create patterns by using the same color yarn. Your color and thread choice can further emphasize the texture.

Imitating textures in pictorial work, like a shingled roof or a lace curtain, requires attention to stitch selection and thread to create both the "feel" and the look in your needlepoint.

Direction of Stitches

The stitch direction will emphasize the way an object is put together. For example, you can create bales of hay or a grassy field by using straight or diagonal stitches.

Changing Tone

Color variations and shading will affect texture. To create the subtly changing colors in a sunset, try using harmonious colors of red: pinks, reds, and oranges.

Raised Effects

You can dramatically change the surface of your needlepoint by using raised stitches for *relief* effects.

Raised stitches form relief effects on their own. Other relief effects can be made by "tramming" your stitches. Trammed pieces can be purchased and come complete with yarn in the correct amounts and colors for completing the piece. Half cross stitch is worked over these long stitches thus creating the padding. If you want to tram your own piece, bring needle with yarn through canvas from right-hand side between the double threads on one row. Carry it across the top of the double mesh and insert at point where the color changes. Then work half cross stitch over the "laid" threads to create a double thickness.

Relief effects are easily created with the velvet stitch. The velvet stitch can be left looped for a fuzzy look or cut for a pile look. For a flower pattern, you can combine a cross stitch for the stem and center of the flower and a velvet stitch that is uncut for the petals. The possibilities are endless!

Needlework 101

Relief is the projection of a figure or part of the ground. In needlepoint, any figure that is raised above the surface of the needlepoint is considered a "relief."

Just Bead It!

Beads give a very special and interesting effect in needlepoint. You can select small detailed areas—use one bead to call attention to the jewel of a wedding ring motif—or edge your design with beads, or cover the entire canvas with them. You'll find that beads come in a huge variety of shapes, sizes, and colors and are available in matte, antique, pearlized, crystal, opaque, and translucent finishes. Lots of scope for the imagination!

You can buy beads at craft shops, specialty bead shops, and needlework shops, and, of course through mail-order and the Internet. See Chapter 7, "Combining Stitches and Special Effects," for more on beadwork.

A Stitch in Time

Be sure to use beads that can be easily threaded, and use a good buttonhole thread to secure them. I suggest that you couch the beads or use the tent stitch. If covering a large area, lay a string of threaded beads on the surface of your needlepoint or canvas and couch the beads at intervals. If you are using beads for details, use the tent stitch by bringing your needle through to the front of the canvas, threading on the bead, and completing the tent stitch in the usual manner. Often stitching through twice (two tents in the same holes) holds the beads well for a snug application.

Touching Up Borders

Borders act like a frame to your piece, and can be solid, patterned, square, oval, round, you name it. Some may be integral parts of the design or just the edging that surrounds the main design or pictorial. Choose a border as you would a picture frame—bold and wide if you want it to be very noticeable and part of the overall design, or narrow and discreet for just an edging to finish off the look. Read on to learn about what types of borders have what effects.

Border Effects

Just by changing the width of your border, you change the whole design. A four-inch border and a one-inch border have dramatically different effects. A wide border becomes a significant part of the overall design, whereas a narrow border allows the motif to have a stronger presence.

And, of course, color plays a role in the effect of the border. You probably have had a similar experience when choosing a frame for a piece of artwork. Do you choose a darker or a lighter frame? You asked yourself which one would show off the artwork the best. Do the same with your needlepoint.

A light- or dark-colored frame can take away from, or call attention to, your main design. Consider these qualities when selecting the type of border for your needlepoint.

Shaped Borders

Stitched borders run the gambit. There are the traditional circles, ovals, and squares, as well as window shapes like *Palladian* or rectangular ones with panes (yes, panes stitched right in the design).

Borders can also be the shape of the design, say a heart, a boat, a vase, or even a star or diamond. More-traditional borders, like rectangles or squares, can be stitched in one color or in geometrics like checks, stripes, diagonal lines, or diamond motifs. Floral motifs worked at intervals make a pretty border and enliven a design.

Needlework 101

Palladian is an architectural term that refers to the style of window that is straight on three sides and arched at the top.

Corners

If you choose to stitch designs in the borders at regular intervals, be sure to consider the corners. You will want to "engineer" your pattern so that the proper number of stitches comes together at the right points. You may want to chart your corner pattern on graph paper before you begin stitching.

Often the corners are a solid color or a single motif like a rose or some type of flower. This way, the sides are easily stitched in a pattern, and you don't have to worry about making your border pattern work in the corners.

Overflowing Borders

When the main design flows into the border or the border is an integral part of the design, the border is considered *overflowing*. The stitches of the main motif become harmonious with the pattern.

An example would be a bouquet of flowers in which the leaves are stitched to appear as if they're falling into the border. You can also reverse that concept, stitching the pattern of the border into the motif.

The Least You Need to Know

➤ Needlepoint backgrounds don't have to be plain; they can be enhanced with fabric, shading, patterns, and beads.

➤ Needlepoint can take on a variety of textures with different combinations of canvas, threads/yarn, and stitches.

➤ Borders act like a frame for your designs. They can be solid, patterned, square, oval, round, or shapes of the design themselves, like a heart, diamond, vase, or star.

Chapter 17

Finishing Your Needlepoint

In This Chapter

➤ Finishing your work with the right tools and with blocking and joining techniques

➤ Mounting and framing your work

➤ Cleaning and repairing needlepoint

Now that you've created a beautiful needlepoint project, and the hard part of designing, stitching, and fretting is over, it's time to finish the job. Like embroidery, your needlepoint will have become distorted while working on it, so you'll need to use the blocking method to get it back into shape. If you are joining the design to something else or wish to frame your work, there are tips and tricks to learn that apply only to needlepoint.

Necessary Tools

Finishing your needlepoint requires you to add a few extra tools to your toolbox: A small tape measure, a hammer, and tacks are items you will need to help you get your needlepoint in shape if any distortion occurred during stitching. You will also need a board that is soft enough to allow tacks to go through it (such as chipboard) and a piece of plastic. You are now ready to "block" your needlepoint. Do you recall from Part 2, "Embroidery Basics," what blocking means? Read on to learn how to apply this technique to needlepoint.

The First Step: Blocking

Blocking, as you learned in embroidery, is a process that stretches your canvas back into its original shape, erasing any distortion that may have occurred during stitching.

This is where your paper or cardboard template of the canvas—the one that you created before you started stitching—comes in handy. Needlepoint is blocked with the stitches face down, unless there are looped stitches that would be crushed during the process. Keep these needlepoints face up and dampen them from the back before tacking down. Apply spray lightly to looped stitched items.

Follow these easy steps to block your needlepoint:

1. Place the needlepoint face down on a soft board with your original canvas template underneath and a piece of plastic between the template and needlepoint. Tape the corners down.

2. Spray the canvas with distilled water or moisten with a sponge.

3. At the center top of the canvas, hammer a tack through the unworked mesh of the canvas (the unworked border). Continue tacking in intervals about one inch apart around needlepoint. Stretch the needlepoint into shape using more spray if necessary and align with the original template.

4. Adjust tacks and stretching until the original shape is achieved.

5. Leave the canvas tacked in place until the canvas is completely dry. It may take days for the needlepoint to dry.

6. For badly distorted pieces, restretch if piece still looks "off" or seems to partially return to preblocked state. You may need to resort to hiring a professional to save your piece if your results are not satisfactory.

A Stitch in Time

Always check your needlepoint before starting the blocking process to make sure that there are no stitches missing from the needlepoint. This is easily done by holding the work up to the light. If you see light, there is a missing stitch.

Joining Needlework Pieces

Sewing sections of needlepoint together is a process called *joining.* Each piece needs to be blocked separately and then "joined" together with a needle and either buttonhole thread or matching yarn.

To join two pieces, first trim both canvas edges to about half an inch. Fold the half-inch edges to the wrong side of the fabric.

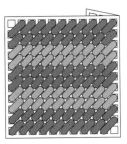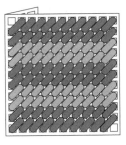

Do not stitch through the turned-back canvas, as this would cause an unnecessary ridge.

With *right* sides together, lay the pieces edge to edge, matching the pattern row by row. Pin and baste together if this will help you keep the pattern straight. Remove the pins before you begin sewing the pieces together on the front side.

Bring the needle up through the first hole of the left-hand piece and insert it down through the first hole of the adjacent piece. Be sure that you secure the tail of the thread in stitching. Then come up in the second hole of the left piece and down into the second hole of the adjacent piece. Continue until the two edges are stitched together. The edges butt against each other and the seam is relatively invisible if the same color thread is used.

If you are joining a piece of fabric to the back of your needlepoint to make a pillow, a sewing machine is fine to use to sew around the joined pieces.

Clever Crafter

Don't always think that the seams shouldn't show! The seams that join sections of needlepoint can be invisible, but, by using contrasting yarns, they can also be a decorative addition to your work.

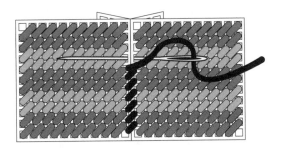

Sometimes by leaving the joining stitches loose and tightening them every five or six laces it is easier to see what you are doing.

Mounting Techniques

Before you frame your work, you will need to mount it on a board to keep it taut and firmly in place. One method is to mount the piece directly onto a board by using the same process you learned in Chapter 9, "The Embroiderer's Finishing Touch." Refer to the section on mounting in Chapter 9 if this is the method that you choose.

Another way is to mount your work on a stretcher. This is the quickest and easiest method of mounting your work. A *stretcher* is a wooden frame over which your needlepoint is stretched and tacked down.

Keeping the needlepoint taut on the stretcher will give the framed piece a more professional look.

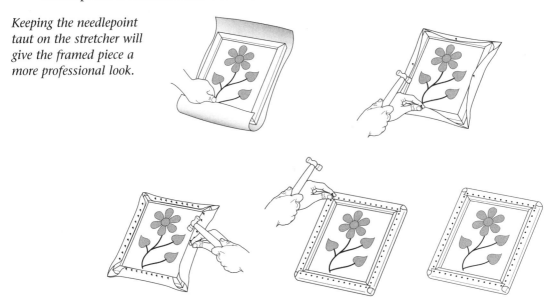

1. First, lay the needlepoint face down and place the stretcher on the back of the needlepoint as if you were going to gift-wrap a present. Fold the unworked areas to the back.

2. Insert a tack in the middle of each side, making sure your needlepoint is positioned correctly with threads at right angles.

3. Tack all around the sides from the center points to the corners, adjusting so that needlepoint is evenly stretched.

4. Miter the unworked corners by folding one corner at a time in toward the piece (it will look like a triangle) and then folding in the two unworked side pieces so that they meet and neatly cover the corner. This is held in place with a tack or a hand-sewn tack.

5. Hammer the tacks in firmly.

Framing Your Work

Framing your needlepoint will give it a permanent resting place, protect it from dust and dirt, and show off your beautiful work to its best advantage.

If you are going to frame it yourself and are using a piece of glass, be sure that the glass does not touch the needlepoint—it will flatten the stitches. Place small strips of wood between the glass and the needlepoint to create space. If you choose to have your work professionally done, your framer will know this.

Some needlepoint pieces look great in a frame without glass, but the only drawback is that dirt and dust collect on these pieces. If you choose this method, periodic cleaning is critical to preserving your work.

A Stitch in Time

You can also hang your needlepoint as a wall tapestry. These pieces need to be lined to maintain the shape of the needlepoint. The lining should be a fabric that is lighter in weight than the needlepoint to allow the work to hang properly. Too heavy a fabric will distort the work. Always prewash fabric so that when you clean your needlepoint, the lining won't shrink.

Hanging Your Needlepoint

Framing isn't your only option for needlepoint. It can also be hung as wall decor. After you have lined the back of the needlepoint, you can choose from several methods for hanging.

One way is to attach a strip of wood the same size as the width of your piece to the top of your needlepoint. To do this, first nail a piece of *Velcro* to the wooden strip, using upholstery tacks. Then sew the matching piece of Velcro to the top of the lined needlework. Screw the wood strip to the wall, and attach the needlework at the top by matching up the Velcro pieces.

Another way is to use curtain hooks and screws to hang your work. Hand-stitch curtain hooks to the back of your lined needlepoint at even intervals, and attach the hooks to screw eyes that have been inserted into the wall at the same intervals as the curtain hooks.

Needlework 101

Velcro is a soft pliable fabric with tiny hooks on the surface that attach to a matching piece with fabric that clings to the hooks.

179

A curtain rod is another choice for hanging your piece. Hand-sew a strip of lining to the top of the lined needlepoint to form a sleeve. Slip a curtain rod through the sleeve, and hang it on the wall with decorative cord.

Instead of a sleeve, you can also sew tabs to slip over the curtain rod. First measure how many tabs you will need for the rod and how long and wide the tabs will be. To create the tabs, cut and sew small pieces of same-sized material to form individual pockets that will hold the rod. You will be folding these tabs lengthwise and widthwise to eliminate raw edges, so make sure you double all measurements. Hem across the width of each tab, and sew the tabs at intervals onto your lining and slip a rod through the tabs. Attach a cord to each end of the rod and hang on the wall.

Decorator's Do's and Don'ts

Do take care when placing your framed work. Don't hang it near heat, in direct sunlight, or in areas of great dampness.

Decorator's Do's and Don'ts

Correctly storing a piece of needlework is just as important as knowing how to display a piece! If you cannot lay it flat, roll it up. Always roll it between acid–free tissue paper and away from sunlight and dust.

Clean but Don't Scrub!

Needlework made of wool can be kept clean fairly easily. Vacuum dust away with a small upholstery attachment. If the threads are silk, dry-clean your piece. If the yarns are colorfast, you may be able to hand-wash your needlework.

Follow these easy steps for hand washing:

1. Use the cotton ball method (see Chapter 9) to check whether the threads are colorfast.

2. Make a paper template of the original size of the needlepoint.

3. Use a container that will accommodate the size of your work.

4. Fill with soapy water (use a soapless quilt "soap") and immerse the needlepoint. If your needlepoint is wool, use cold water to avoid shrinkage. Or roll in damp towel instead of immersion. If you are worried about shrinkage, have your needlepoint professionally dry-cleaned.

5. Let needlepoint soak and press gently. Drain and rinse in clean water until rinse water is clear.

6. Lay needlepoint flat with right side up, and blot up excess water with a clean, dry sponge.

7. Reblock the piece, using the instructions given earlier in this chapter.

Decorator's Do's and Don'ts

Do not use a metal bowl to clean your needlework in! Sometimes metal can react negatively with colors, which could ruin your design.

A Stitch in Time

Treat stained needlepoints as you would your fine clothing. Check a cleaning guide on how to remove different types of spot stains. If needleworks are very badly stained, ask a professional cleaner how to save the work.

The Least You Need to Know

➤ Blocking is a process that returns your canvas to its original shape and eliminates any distortion that may have occurred during stitching.

➤ With the joining method, you can hand-sew sections of needlepoint together.

➤ Before you can frame your work, you will need to mount it on a board to keep it taut and firmly in place.

➤ Framing your needlepoint lengthens its life by protecting it from dust and dirt and turns your work into framed art that you can admire daily!

➤ Cleaning your needlework is critical for preserving your hard work.

Chapter 18

An Easy Needlepoint Project from Start to Finish

In This Chapter

➤ Start small—making a dollhouse rug

➤ Preparation is the best way to start any project

➤ Use graphs to design your own patterns

As a novice, it's good to begin with small projects. You may not be ready to make a 9-by-12-foot needlepoint rug, but a dollhouse rug is a fine place to start. If you or your child don't have a dollhouse, consider giving the rug away as a gift to a niece or grandchild or to someone you know who is a dollhouse hobbyist.

This chapter will take you step by step, from the materials needed to get started to advice on finishing the project, with plenty of helpful hints along the way. I'll also show you how to use graph paper to design your own patterns.

All the information that you learned in the earlier chapters on needlepoint will be refreshed by the act of doing and stitching with your own two hands. Clear instructions will make your first needlepoint project fun and easy!

Making a Dollhouse Rug

A dollhouse rug is a perfect choice for your first needlepoint piece. It is a small, simple project that you can begin and finish with ease. This project will ready you for other projects like pillows and wall decor.

The color key for your rug is made up of symbols that match the symbols on the rug chart.

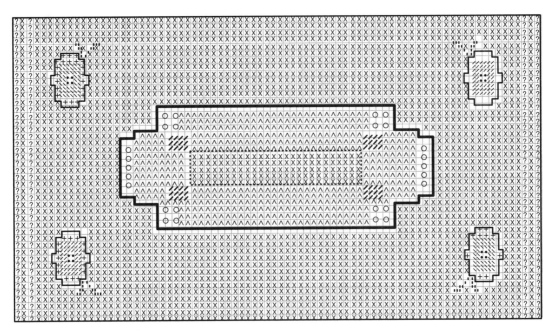

A dollhouse rug to stitch.

Key to Colors	
O	Salmon
+	Red
/	Yellow
?	Gold
^	Bright blue
X	Pale blue

Getting Acquainted with the Materials

Start your project by getting a feel for your materials. How the yarn is threaded through the eye of the needle, how the yarn and needle work through the canvas, and how you hold your canvas—these are all new concepts until you start and get used to the materials and stitches.

Materials needed:

➤ 12-count double (Penelope) canvas cut 10 inches by 6 inches

➤ No. 18 tapestry needle

➤ Wool tapestry yarn in six colors (check key), one skein each color, except two of pale blue

➤ Piece of blue felt to cover the back, cut approximately 8 inches by 4 inches

➤ Blue cotton thread

➤ Masking tape

Clever Crafter

Chart your monogram on a rug, or if you needlepoint one for a friend, chart your friend's monogram. There is nothing more treasured than a personalized gift.

The Canvas

For your miniature rug, you'll need double canvas (12 threads per inch). This mesh is made of pairs of threads, and you will work your stitches over the pairs. Be sure to tape the canvas edges with masking tape to prevent fraying. Your rug will be approximately 7½ inches in length and 3½ inches in width when finished.

The Needle

You will be using a tapestry (blunt-tipped) needle, since your stitches will be placed in the holes in the canvas and you will not need to pierce the canvas threads with a sharp needle. A number 18 tapestry needle has a large round eye for easy threading and will comfortably fit through the mesh holes without distorting the canvas.

Decorator's Do's and Don'ts

Don't start and end your threads in the same place! The extra thickness will form an unsightly ridge.

The Yarn

For this rug, the type of yarn and colors will effect the final look. The colors are specified in the materials list and the type of yarn is as well. You will use wool tapestry yarn, which is a single-strand yarn. It is slightly finer than three strands of Persian yarn. Colors of yarn are specified in the materials list and in the color key. Feel free to experiment with other colors.

Cut the yarn into 18-inch lengths to prevent it from fraying while you are pulling it through the canvas mesh holes.

Remember that if the yarn becomes twisted while you are needlepointing, drop the needle and let it hang. The yarn will untwist by itself. Don't try to stitch with twisted yarn; it will appear thin and will not cover the fabric.

The Chart

The chart is illustrated on graph paper in the previous figure, using symbols to guide you with the correct color yarn. This rug is done in six colors to form a pretty pattern. Each symbol also represents a stitch on the chart. By stitching in the corresponding holes on the canvas, your rug will start to take shape.

The Stitch

Use the tent stitch on the entire rug. Refer to Chapter 13, "Just Point and Stitch," to refresh your memory on this basic stitch. It is worked in a small diagonal, always slanting in the same direction. You will become familiar with the needle, canvas, and yarn all working together.

185

Ready to Start

Before you begin stitching, keep in mind the following tips:

➤ Begin stitching from the center of the design and work outward.

➤ Use one strand of tapestry yarn in the designated color that is listed on the key.

➤ Secure tail of yarn with beginning stitches and end tail with last stitches.

➤ Use the tent stitch to cover one intersection of the canvas threads that correspond to the symbol on the chart.

➤ Count your stitches frequently to eliminate the chances of making a mistake.

Finishing

When you have stitched the design, including the background, your rug is almost finished. If any distortion occurred, you will need to block your rug before attaching the felt backing. Refer to Chapter 17, "Finishing Your Needlepoint," for a refresher. If very little distortion occurred, steam the back of the rug with an iron and leave it to dry thoroughly. Trim the canvas edges to ½ inch. Turn these back onto the wrong side, miter the corners, and lightly steam with an iron; wait for them to dry in place.

Trace the final measurement of the rug, and cut a piece of felt just slightly smaller than the pattern. Using the blue cotton thread, sew the felt onto the back of the rug with a simple slip stitch around the edges, attaching the felt and the canvas edges.

The slip stitch should be invisible on the felt and rug. Pick up a thread or two of the canvas mesh on back side of folded edges and then run the needle through the underside of the felt just catching a small piece. Continue to catch the inside fold of the mesh and the underside of the felt first on one side, then the other.

Voilà! You have completed your first needlework.

Where to Go from Here?

Now that you have finished your rug, you have a good sense of the time that it takes to complete a canvas of this size. You also have a feel for the tension of the yarn, stitches, and canvas. The more needlepoint you do, the better you will become at it.

If you have a dollhouse, you can immediately give your rug a home. If not, you may wish to give it as a gift. Or, you may want to use the graph paper, make your own designs, and try to sell these little creations! Whichever you choose to do, you have created a fine piece of needlework and you can be proud to have completed a hand-stitched piece all on your own!

Grids to Make Your Own

After you complete your rug, you may want to strike out on your own and use the following sheets of graph paper to sketch your own patterns and designs. Feel free to practice more rugs or try out other designs that you just can't wait to start stitching.

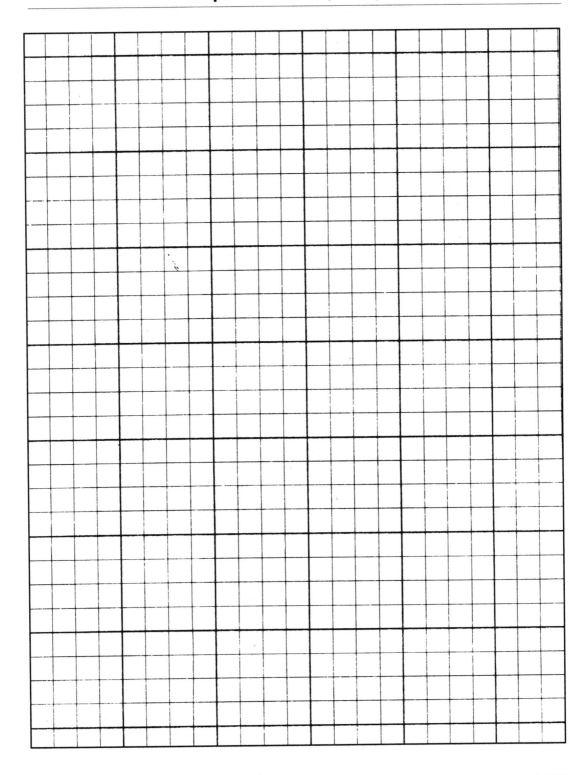

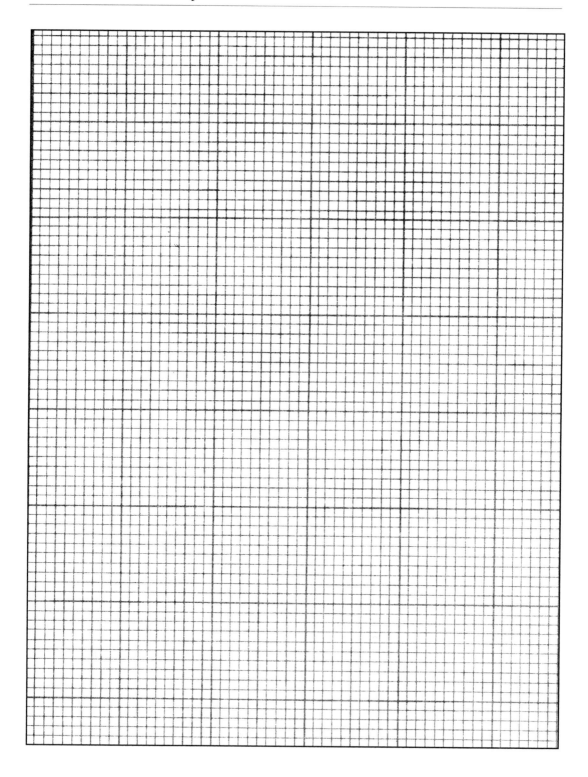

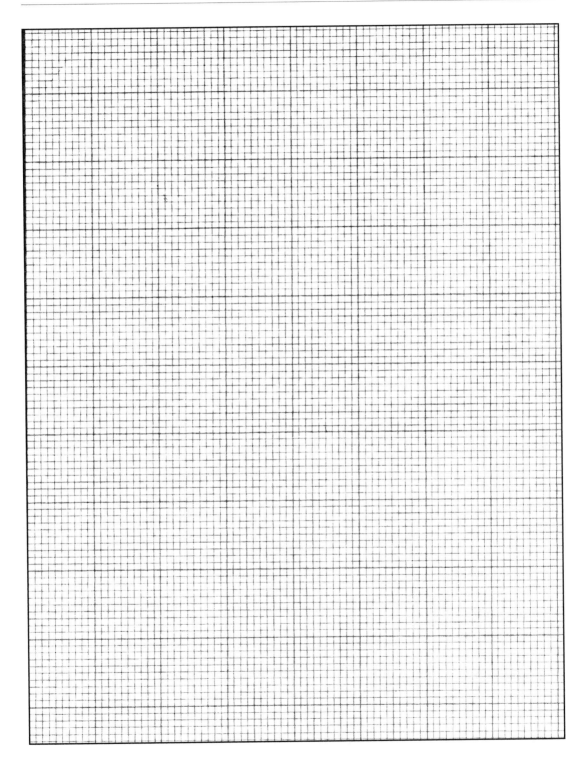

The Least You Need to Know

➤ Small projects are a good start for novice needlepointers. A dollhouse rug is a perfect choice.

➤ Getting a feel for your materials is a good place to start for your first needlework. Understanding how the needle, yarn, and canvas work together is key.

➤ Preparing your materials ahead of time is a step toward a successful needlepoint project.

➤ Graph paper is a great tool for charting your own designs.

Part 6

Getting Crafty

This how-to guide would not be complete without giving you insight into all aspects of the needlecraft world. Peruse these chapters for ways to take the craft to a new level and how to share your new hobby with others. Needlepoint and embroidery are wonderful ways to create gifts for friends and family as well as beautiful items for your home.

But needlework doesn't have to be a solitary craft. Get involved with craft groups, sell your work, or teach the craft to others. Put the most into your new hobby, and you'll be amazed at what you get in return!

Chapter 19

Beyond Needle and Thread

In This Chapter

➤ Finding perseverance and a positive attitude for your new hobby

➤ Making time for needleworking

➤ Taking comfort in needlework

➤ Sharing your skill with others

You've bought this book and read this far, so it's safe to assume that you've decided that needlework is the hobby for you! A new hobby is like a new toy. When you first pick it up, you are anxious to learn everything about it! For needleworking, "everything" includes mastering the basics, acquiring practical knowledge about your tools, finding out how quickly you catch on, judging how much time it will take you to master some areas, and deciding whether you will keep needlework as a lifetime art.

As you devour everything about your new hobby that you can get your hands on, there are things in this chapter that will help you take your craft further than your needle and thread. You'll learn other tips, psychology of the craft, and where to join up with others to share your new hobby. You may even feel good enough about your newly acquired talent to send off a sample to a magazine. What if your first tries are so-so, should you keep going or start all over again? And how do you come up with enough time to engage in your new hobby? This chapter can shed some light on these and other questions to keep you going in the right direction.

Perseverance in a New Hobby

Starting a new craft or hobby requires a mind-over-matter attitude. If you think you can do something, you usually can. Try to gather as much information on the subject of needlework as possible. Read everything you can—as they say, "Reading is knowledge!" And with knowledge comes confidence in your subject, which in turn makes you want to know and *do* more. Doing gives you experience, and practice makes you good at what you do. The more you do, the more mistakes you will make and that's when you learn the most. Never be afraid of trying new stitches and techniques. You might mess up on the first few tries, but you will get it right if you persevere and keep a positive attitude.

Seek advice if you can't do a technique properly. Call an expert at your local stitchery shop, or get on the Internet and get involved in a chat session (see the section later in this chapter on sharing ideas) to ask about your problem areas. Most of all, keep going!

Never Give Up!

So your first stab at needlepoint wasn't perfect. Should you then just give up? No! You join the club—the "First-Timers Anonymous Club"—that every novice needle-worker belonged to when she (or he!) first took up the craft. Soon you will graduate and move on, but not before making your share of mistakes and blunders!

I have even kept my first needlepoint pieces, which I did as a little girl. Imperfect projects have inherent charm—they say that you are human and just beginning. First projects are good to look at periodically to show you how far you have come. Your progression as a needleworker is documented over time. You see how your tastes have changed, how your choices of colors and patterns have sorted out over time. So you see, you can use your first needlepoint, as well as those that follow, as a reference. And don't be afraid to display them, too!

If you are a perfectionist and can't live with mistakes, you have two choices. You can either remove stitches and redo them, a painstaking but ultimately satisfying task, or you can ask for help, a path that often yields a bounty of useful information. If you choose to remove stitches, do not reuse the yarn. Once yarn or thread is stitched, it curls and becomes difficult to work the second time.

If you do not know what you are doing wrong, enlist the help of that fabulous needleworker aunt of yours or the local stitchery shop owner. March right into the shop, and tell her you will be a devoted customer of hers if she helps you out! That way you won't give up if you know that you can rely on someone's help. Remember, most shop owners and staff are delighted to help customers; after all, they love needlework themselves and want to share their enthusiasm. A quick question from a customer is not a problem, but it's unreasonable to expect the shop owner to drop everything to help you with a complicated question on a crowded Saturday morning, when you bring in a project that you have purchased at a competing store, or when you arrive five minutes before the shop closes and want to change 40 colors. If you need extensive help, some shops set aside certain days for questions. Or you can set up an appointment, or return at a less-busy hour. Patience and courtesy go a long way in these situations.

Making Time for Your New Craft

People who complete their needlework are the type of people who find time for their hobby. You say that you have no time? As I say to people who claim they have no time for exercise, "Make time!" Make time for your new hobby, and you will get the most from it. The best part about needlework as a hobby is that you can take it with you wherever you go—in a car, on a train, on a plane ….

Just think of the hours or even half-hours that are available to you when you are waiting in lines, waiting for the train, idling away a lunch hour, talking on the phone, watching TV, riding in the car, or taking the bus. Waiting for your daughter's piano lesson to finish, sitting in a two-hour traffic jam, or being stuck on a delayed train—these minutes can become a productive use of your time. You'd be amazed how fast those delays go by when your hands and mind are busy!

Whatever your lifestyle, you can find time. Keep your projects portable and handy. Keep one in the car so you can't make any excuse about forgetting it. Put it in your purse along with your checkbook, license, and cell phone, and you're sure not to forget it.

The Comfort of Needlework

Needlework can be just the hobby that you have been looking for. Needlework is very soothing. It keeps your hands busy while it relaxes you with the rhythm of pulling the thread through the fabric. Your mind is alert as you keep track of the pattern, but the irritations of daily life recede as you concentrate on your piece. Often in times of stress you may fret and not know what to do with yourself. Needlework provides quiet time for thinking, creating, and accomplishing. Needlework is often prescribed for people who need to redirect their lives, impart some sense of calm, and work toward a goal.

Scientists measured the healthful effects of five different hobby-type activities requiring hand-eye coordination: playing bridge, doing crossword puzzles, painting, and cross-stitching (I can't recall the fifth). Anyway, the researchers measured blood pressure, heart rate, perspiration rate, and respiration rate. They discovered that cross stitchers experienced the greatest drop in all those measurements, close to a 20-point drop in blood pressure for experienced stitchers, and equally dramatic drops for other rates.

It's also very satisfying to complete a project on your own. Whether you are designing your own canvas or stitching a kit, there is a great satisfaction in creating something that is homemade. You feel proud of your project … so much so that you may give it

197

as a gift to someone special. Making other people happy is all a part of making yourself feel happy.

If you choose to take classes, you will meet new friends who like to chat about needlework, give tips, and discuss designs. This is also great if you are new to a community and looking for people who have similar interests.

Sharing Ideas

One of the most uplifting parts about needlework is the camaraderie with other needlework enthusiasts. Joining a craft group or starting your own is a place where people with similar interests can come together and share their personal experiences in needlework. Or you may want to share from your desk at home by chatting online with people you don't even know!

You may become so adept at your hobby that you will want to share your ideas with the world in a magazine article. Or you may simply be satisfied sharing your knowledge with your local community by helping the elderly with projects or starting a new generation of needleworkers by teaching children.

Joining or Starting a Craft Group

One of the best ways to learn more about your needlework hobby and to share your thoughts and ideas is through a craft group that meets weekly or monthly. Beginners as well as veterans on the subject of needlework come together and discuss projects, different techniques, the latest gadgets, and what is going on in the world of needlework. Beginners learn from the more seasoned needleworkers who are eager to pass on their knowledge.

You may meet at the church hall, a community room at the public library, the leader's home, the lobby of an inn, or anywhere needleworkers can come together. Your local stitchery shop owner may also be able to refer you to a local meeting place.

If there isn't a local group, why not start one yourself? Post ads on billboards, or ask your stitchery shop to post a notice. An ad in the local paper could work well, too. You could suggest a needlework get-together in which everyone takes a turn sponsoring the group at her home, complete with refreshments. Do whatever it takes to keep the wonderful world of needlework alive!

There is also an unparalleled resource for adventures in all types of embroidery, including needlepoint. Its goal is to further embroidery through education of its members and the public and through public service. Membership encompasses all skill levels, from the newest beginner through the professional textile artist and internationally known teachers of embroidery arts. Local chapters offer newsletters and mini classes throughout the year for local members and also help sponsor state, regional, and national workshops and correspondence courses. Dues are approximately $35 per year (varies a bit by chapter) and include both local and national membership, plus a quarterly needlework magazine. If you need help or if your husband's eyes glaze over when you start talking about needlework, this is the place to find congenial and sympathetic companions.

Chatting Online

If you can't get out of the house but are dying to "talk needlework," chat online. Chat on what? Online. On the Internet. Yes, you can dial up a great chat session on www.needlepoint.about.com and have a conversation with your fellow Internet needlework buddies. The chat session on the about.com Web site is on Monday evenings between 8:00 and 9:00 P.M Eastern standard time. Surf the Net and learn more about needlework, and share your ideas with the world without leaving your chair.

Submitting Designs to Magazines

Think you may have mastered your craft and want to submit your work to a well-known magazine? Check Appendix A, "Resources for Novice Needleworkers," and Appendix B, "Supplies: A Local and Global Source Guide," for magazines that might be interested in you. If you do submit to a magazine, make sure you are sending your embroidery work to a magazine devoted to embroidery and not needlepoint, and vice versa. Spend some time checking out the right magazines, and you won't waste time and money having your work sent back!

Open the magazine and find the masthead, which contains the list of the people who work at and run the magazine. See who is the needlepoint or embroidery editor (may be the same person), and find the address of the publication. Send a color photograph or a colored photocopy of the pieces that you wish to submit, along with a brief resumé and a letter stating your desire to be included in an issue.

Now all you can do is wait and see what happens! You can follow up with a phone call a week or so after the magazine has received your package. If they accept your ideas and want to "shoot" (photograph) your work, they will give you a call and discuss the details with you. Often magazines will pay you to include your work in an issue. Usually the sum is small, from $50 to $200.

Getting your work in a magazine can be exciting and a real confidence booster. Just think, you will be sharing your ideas with its subscribers! Ask what its circulation is to get a rough estimate of how many people will view your work and how much sharing you'll be doing!

Volunteering with Children ... Sharing and Winning

The best way to keep the art of needlework alive is to teach another generation of needlework enthusiasts. Kids love to learn, but you have to love teaching. If you've picked up this craft and want to share what you've learned, that's all you need for qualifications!

You can call the local school and volunteer for a one-time class or a series of after-school classes, or you could have a stitching party in your home once a week. The local Brownie or Girl Scout troop may need you to teach needlework to the children so that they can earn a badge. This will give you an opportunity to share your ideas with children who might not have any form of needlework in their lives. It could inspire the kids to explore the world of arts and crafts, opening a new world to them. Crafts keep children focused and bring them happiness and feelings of accomplishment. Crafts develop dexterity skills, teach children to follow directions, and show them how to *create*.

So much can come from sharing your ideas and volunteering your time. And what do you get out of all this? You get to know that you have given back, touched lives that may never have been inspired, and released feelings of sheer joy. Wow!

Help Out at Nursing Homes

On the other end of the spectrum, why not volunteer at a nursing home in your area? Many lifelong needleworkers, and some that have never picked up a needle and thread, could be uplifted just by your presence, and certainly by your sharing of time and enthusiasm about needlework. Some nursing home patients may enjoy a little help with their stitching if their hands are stiff and feeble. Others will just appreciate attention and the idea of learning a new hobby in their golden years. Again, it is a win-win situation—the patients are active and happy, and you are giving to your community in a very thoughtful way by sharing your time and knowledge.

Look in the Yellow Pages for the names of some of the nursing homes in your area. It could be the brightest part of the patients' day, and yours!

The Least You Need to Know

➤ Starting a new craft or hobby requires a positive attitude and perseverance!

➤ People who complete their needlework projects are the type of people who make time for their hobby.

➤ Needlework is very soothing. It keeps your hands pleasantly active and your mind calmed and relaxed.

➤ You can keep needlework alive by sharing your ideas locally and globally.

Chapter 20

More Than
a Hobby

In This Chapter

➤ Giving away your work

➤ Determining whether selling your work is for you

➤ Finding your market and selling at craft fairs and on the Internet

---

So, by now your house is filled with the fruits of your labor. You have cross-stitched pillows, embroidered curtains, and monogrammed your teenager's underwear. (I said "fruits of labor" not Fruit of the Loom!) Well, maybe you haven't had the time to get into the craft this extensively yet, but when you do you may find enjoyment in taking your skill beyond the front door.

There are several ways to use this new craft as gifts and for profit. A handmade wedding sampler is a more-treasured gift than a salad spinner. Once you start giving away your work as gifts, you'll never go back to the store! Or, you may also develop an interesting look to your designs or create a new product that could sell at craft fairs or among acquaintances. If you get really handy and like to teach, start up a summer stitching class for the neighborhood kids. Their parents will love you!

The more you get into needlework, the more you'll find yourself being led in certain directions by your craft. Go with it! Whichever direction your needlework takes you is worth exploring.

Give It Away

I'm sure you've already thought of some gifts that you can create with your new craft—and perhaps they're already completed. Maybe you even took up needleworking so that you could make gifts for loved ones. That's great!

As I've said before, once you start giving gifts you'll never look back. Sure, you won't give embroideries or needlepoint on every occasion, but isn't it wonderful to have the option?

When making gifts for people, be sure to give yourself enough time. If you are embroidering pillowcases for an upcoming wedding, calculate backward from the wedding date how much time you'll need to complete the project. Then double it! You never know what can happen between now and an occasion. Most people will understand if you tell them that a handmade gift will be late, but finishing gifts on time is much more rewarding!

In choosing what to make, consider the giftee. If you don't know their tastes, find out by snooping around with their family and friends. If it's a home item, come up with an excuse to visit so you can get an idea of their color schemes and tastes. Don't make them a tea cozy if they don't drink tea! If they have just moved into a new home, needlepoint an image of their new house!

If you're going to put time into a gift, try to personalize it as much as you can. Your giftees will appreciate your efforts that much more!

Selling Your Work

Don't be too shy if you are really serious about selling your work. The nice thing about a craft is that it sells itself, but only if you are willing to display it.

If you've never sold anything before, be prepared. Research is your best tool in this case. You may create really cool embroidered Post-It Note holders, but will anyone buy them? Check out your market and see what is selling at other craft shows. You need to make items that consumers are looking to buy. Also, creating items that interest you will help you to enjoy your work and make them easier to sell.

Is Selling for You?

Before you put items on a craft table, though, put your work and yourself to the test by asking yourself the following questions:

> ➤ **What do I enjoy stitching?** Let's say the hottest-selling item is cross-stitched toaster covers. You hate making toaster covers, but you see your friend Sally cashing in with hers at craft fairs. You decide to make a couple yourself, which sell easily, but now you find that you don't even look forward to picking up a needle and thread. Certainly, there's nothing wrong with creating something to fit the market—all the best entrepreneurs have done it—but keep your goals in

check. Alternate stitching toaster covers with samplers, something you do enjoy. Just remember that if you don't enjoy what you're doing, soon you won't do it at all!

➤ **The toughest question of all: Is my stuff sellable?** This is a hard question to ask yourself, but it's the most important. To get the answer, go to craft fairs, peruse magazines, join a craft group, and watch what other people produce. Does your work look professional? If you are not at the stage where your work is polished or close to looking polished, wait to start selling your wares. Spend some more time fine-tuning your craft, and then hit the market!

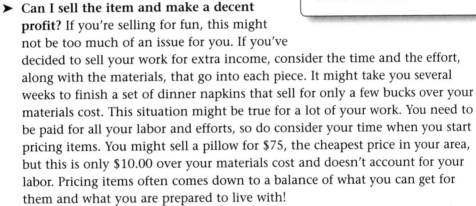

A Stitch in Time

The best-selling needleworks show consumers' wants and needs. How do you find out what's "hot"? Spend some time at craft fairs and small shops that sell gift items. Find out which items sell out. Take notes on displays and on how the seller interacts with customers.

➤ **Can I sell the item and make a decent profit?** If you're selling for fun, this might not be too much of an issue for you. If you've decided to sell your work for extra income, consider the time and the effort, along with the materials, that go into each piece. It might take you several weeks to finish a set of dinner napkins that sell for only a few bucks over your materials cost. This situation might be true for a lot of your work. You need to be paid for all your labor and efforts, so do consider your time when you start pricing items. You might sell a pillow for $75, the cheapest price in your area, but this is only $10.00 over your materials cost and doesn't account for your labor. Pricing items often comes down to a balance of what you can get for them and what you are prepared to live with!

➤ **Do I have the time for this?** You might be gung-ho at the beginning but soon find out that you don't have the time to crank out enough pieces to sell. What if your work really takes off and you start getting orders? Will you have the time to fill them? Make sure that you can set aside time in your week—or even every day—to do needlework. Try setting up a schedule every Friday and write in the times you will devote to projects in the coming week. You'll be more motivated to pick up your workbasket, and, after a few weeks, you'll also get a better idea of how long it takes to complete projects.

➤ **Do I have the means to sell the items?** Craft fairs and word of mouth will become your best friends. If you live in a remote area, the Internet might be a good outlet for you. However, keep in mind that even though the Net is popular for buying and selling items, people still want to see what they are buying close up with their own eyes, and even touch it with their hands. Talk to craft store owners and local craft organizations. Look in your Sunday newspaper and places that you know hold large events. The more people you talk to, the more you'll find out.

However you approach the selling of your wares, remember to have fun with it. Selling your work can be very fulfilling and a great way to meet people!

Determining Your Market

Who will be buying your work? Let's face it, you just won't sell that many embroidered bow ties to men. Some men may buy needlework items, but women are still the major needlework consumers. Who are these buyers? I don't mean "who" as in a list of names you can sell to. I mean "who" as in the market segment to which your work will appeal. Are they people who prefer *Country Living* looks or off-beat designs?

Your style will attract a market of people with the same style, and maybe a few buyers looking for different items to shake up their decor. The most important thing to keep in mind is to create what interests you and then find customers with the same tastes.

Reaching those customers is another ball of yarn. Sometimes it's easy. Art and craft shows may be enough for you, especially if your work has a popular, mainstream look. You may want to advertise in particular magazines or on the Internet, or attend shows in a different state (or area of your state) where you'll find a bigger population of your customer type. Keep in mind that finding your customers is really up to you; you can't depend on them finding you—especially if you don't make yourself and your craft known. Visibility is everything. If customers don't know you exist, how can they buy up your stuff?

Where to Sell Your Wares

You will need to decide what is the best outlet to sell your wares. You may have time to go to craft fairs and set up a table. Maybe the little shop in your neighborhood is the best spot for your goods. Even the Internet may give you global exposure. Consider the research that you have done on marketing your work and decide which will be the best sales tool for you.

Craft Fairs

How crafty is your area? Crafts are big in just about every corner of the globe, so finding fairs in which to sell your work should not be too difficult.

Almost every community has craft fairs. To find out the when and where for local craft fairs, ask other needleworkers and people active in town affairs, such as someone who works in the town's recreation department. For larger events in the bigger cities, look in magazines, and on the Net, and contact the chamber of commerce for crafting organizations listed in your area.

Craft fairs will charge you a fee for a spot to display your work. Smaller fairs will be cheap, probably under $30, but the larger fairs can charge several hundred dollars or more. Sometimes they provide a table, and sometimes it's up to you to bring all of the equipment. It's always better to be prepared to lug your own stuff, just in case.

Some items to bring should include …

➤ Price tags and markers

➤ At least $50 (in ones, fives, tens, and coins)

➤ A safe place to keep money

➤ Business cards (these can be made up cheaply)

➤ Calculator

➤ Receipt book (or use plain paper)

➤ Extra paper for taking orders

➤ Plastic bags for purchased items and garbage

➤ A chair (for you!)

➤ Tables and screens to display work, and tacks or nails and a hammer

Don't forget to make a sign, too! The more professional your display looks, the more customers will stop to browse. It's also a good idea to have a separate sign saying that you will do custom work. Some customers may not realize that they want their favorite lighthouse embroidered until you put the idea in their heads!

Before you go to the craft fair, decide whether you will include taxes in your prices or will add the taxes separately. If you charge separately for the taxes, make a list of what the taxes are for a purchase of $10 and up. You will need a retail license to sell taxable items. This is available through your state's department of taxation.

Also, bring along some things to make your work stand out, like holiday lights (get the battery-operated kind), display shelving, fabric for an attractive backdrop, or anything eye-catching that you can drape among your hanging work.

A Stitch in Time

Find a partner! Sharing a table at a craft fair has a lot of advantages. You can split the cost, take breaks without having to "close shop," and have someone to talk to during the dead spots. Plus, if your partner creates different kinds of work, you will have a more varied and inviting display!

Decorator's Do's and Don'ts

Stay away from flea markets! Well, flea markets themselves are great, but for selling your work they're not the best outlet. Most people going to flea markets are looking for antiques and old cheap "stuff" for a few dollars. Don't waste your day here—save it for an arts and crafts fair where the clientele is expecting to pay for good work.

Some craft shows are juried. The exhibitor must submit samples, which are then judged for suitability in comparison with the products of other exhibitors. Generally, a juried show is a good thing because the wares are of high quality and often of unique design. Customers are willing to pay higher prices for these premium items.

Mom-and-Pop Shops

There are some great small stores that sell primarily gift items. Thank goodness the "-marts" haven't totally taken over the small shops yet!

These shops love selling items from the locals, particularly if you live in a tourist town. Talk to several of the shops in your area and find out, first, if they're interested in your work and, second, how they operate. Do they charge you for space? Do they get a commission on each item of yours that they sell? You'll find that these shops typically utilize the commission route because it brings in more money.

Also find out how much space in a display case or on a table they can offer you. Or, find out where in the store your items will be displayed. Displaying your work there might not be worth it if you're tucked in a back corner! Work with shop owners as much as you can. If they're geared more toward seasonal merchandise, make sure you offer to create holiday items or a variety of work throughout the year so they won't get bored with your stock. Small shop owners are usually willing to work with you if they like your stuff! Also be sure to ask if you can put out business cards—for all the customers who like your stuff!

Decorator's Do's and Don'ts

Unless you have a very good reason, don't turn down a shop owner once you have committed to displaying your work in that shop! If you turn down the offer, you've closed a door of opportunity. Go to your favorite shop first, and then work your way down the list. You might get rejected, so be prepared for that too!

Selling on the Internet

Starting from scratch on the Internet is like searching for a fine-gauge embroidery needle in a really, really large haystack. Just for a half-second of fun, type in "embroidery" as a keyword search. You'll come up with endless screens of home pages, mixed in with major Web sites on the subject. Some Internet providers (like AOL or Netscape) will show different search results.

The biggest thing to know about your customers is that they are like other sellers' customers. People who search the Internet are looking for things that interest them. Whether you decide to sell your items on your own home page or on someone else's Web site, you will still have to work at reaching your audience. Don't think that you will instantly get customers once you post something on the Web. It's just too big of a world now! People might stumble onto your stuff, but only if they have been poking around needlework Web sites to begin with.

The best way to get the word out about your items on the Web is to "cross-promote." If you have business cards, print your Web address on the card. If you have a mailbox that is near the road, attach a sign that hangs below your mailbox that advertises your needlework and your Web site. Anyone driving by will view it. Go on other Web sites and find out if you can make trades: Swap a mention of each other's Web site. Advertise in your local newspaper.

The Internet is a great place to conduct business, but it shouldn't be the only place. One thing the Net hasn't replaced is one-on-one contact. If you're really serious about selling your work, a Web site or home page is a good tool. The only drawback is that your goods cannot be touched or seen in full view. Some customers will want to see the handmade quality and be able to see the colors in person.

Clever Crafter

You may want to begin by entering your work in the home arts division of the local fair, right down the row from the prized tomatoes and the best blueberry pie. You never know—you may come home with a blue ribbon. And that's one credential to add to your resumé!

Exploring Other Crafts

The best salespeople are the most knowledgeable salespeople. The more you know about the subject of needlework, not just needlepoint and embroidery, the more you can show your confidence in your subject and work, which is key to any customers gaining confidence in you!

Of course your enthusiasm for embroidery and needlepoint will most definitely lead you to want to explore other kinds of needlework. Quilting is a natural go-together with embroidery and of course rug hooking is fun, as well as knitting and crocheting. The more needlework you learn about and try, the more you will know about the subject and the better a salesperson you will be at the fairs. Your displays will be full of your handiwork, and they will show that you are a needlework devotee and serious businessperson!

The Least You Need to Know

➤ Making gifts for others can be rewarding as well as challenging. Make sure you give yourself more than enough time to complete the project.

➤ Before selling your work, determine whether you're ready to devote the time, money, and effort.

➤ Find out what items you would like to sell and how you will get your items into the marketplace.

➤ Don't forget to explore other types of needlework. You will gain knowledge and expertise—good attributes to help sales!

Resources for Novice Needleworkers

If you need help in your quest to learn more about needlework resources, this appendix is for you! From free catalogs to class sessions, education beyond the basics is as easy as leafing through, reading from, walking through, or calling up! Most resources are closer and more easily accessible than you think.

If you are lucky enough to be hooked up to the Internet, a huge resource awaits you. In surfing the Web, you can explore endless possibilities and do all of your shopping without even getting out of your chair!

Mail-Order Catalogs

Despite the current Internet frenzy, there are still ways to order items the old-fashioned way—on paper! You might be surprised at the enormous amount of merchandise available through mail-order catalogs for needlework lovers like you. From thread to needles to kits to books, catalogs are packed with items to satisfy every taste and budget. Many catalogs are free, but some companies charge a few dollars to get you on their list. Many mail-order catalogs arrive in your mailbox with a couple of periodic-sale catalogs interspersed.

When ordering from a catalog, be sure to note the catalog company's return policy and shipping charges, just in case you decide to return your goods because of wrong colors or because something wasn't what you expected.

Most mail-order companies offer express or air delivery, customer service hotlines, and refund policies. Full-service catalogs may also have a framing service, complete finishing service, and special commissions. A finishing service will make your needlework into a piece of home decor such as a pillow or footstool cover. You just do the stitching for your pattern, and they will take care of the rest. Special commissions are custom designs in which a particular pattern is designed especially for you—such as your coat of arms on a seat cover that will fit that odd-shaped antique chair!

The best needlework catalogs for you carry your personal tastes, kits at your level of needlework, and prices that fit your budget. Remember that you aren't required to use a project exactly as it's shown in a catalog. You might want to fashion your work into a pillow instead of framing it, as a project suggests. Also, you might not like the frame that is shown with a design. Change it! This will help your own style come through. Most catalogs are artfully presented and can actually help you see their goods' intended use and how they are incorporated into a beautiful room. To help you find a catalog to suit your needs and tastes, consider a couple of my of my favorites for framing, pillows, rugs, belts, and accessories:

Erica Wilson
717 Madison Avenue
New York, NY 10021
1-800-97-ERICA

A New York–based designer with fine patterns for needlepoint, some included in The Metropolitan Museum of Art.

Glorafilia
Unit 52 No. 2 Mill
Halliwell Industrial Estate
Rossini Street
Bolton
Lancashire
London
BL1 8DL
Phone: 0181 906 0213

A London-based designer needlepoint company, Glorafilia has a full-service catalog specializing in pillows, samplers, rugs, bell pulls, and special commissions.

Magazines: Inexpensive Needlework Sessions

Many excellent needlework publications are available these days. Some are aimed strictly at beginners or at advanced stitchers; others offer projects for a variety of abilities. Browse through several different magazines (try the public library) to see which ones suit your style and interests. Purchase a copy of the one that you like the most; perhaps you will want to treat yourself to a subscription. Note how often the magazine is published. This can vary from monthly to quarterly or only annually.

Inside the needlework magazine you will find projects and patterns, interviews with designers, product news, books of interest, letters from readers with needlework questions, and upcoming needlework events. Needlework shops often advertise in these magazines, and the ads are a good source for locating shops across the country. (Also see Appendix B, "Supplies: A Local and Global Source Guide," for more information about magazines as sources.) Explicit directions, with colors and thread or yarn requirements, will be given for each project. Historical information on different needlework subjects is often explored, and particular stitches or techniques might be discussed.

A particularly good publication with a wide range of needle-art projects is *Inspirations,* printed in South Australia. Here are addresses for a variety of publications:

Beautiful Cross Stitch
2211 N. Elston Ave.
Chicago, IL 60614
Phone: 773-278-5695

New Zealand publication distributed by Quilters' Resource, Inc.

Inspirations
2211 N. Elston Ave.
Chicago, IL 60614
Phone: 773-278-5695

South Australian needlework publication distributed by Quilters' Resource, Inc., with high-caliber and beautiful work patterns.

Piecework
Chicago, IL 60614
Phone: 1-800-676-6543

Features all types of needlework with patterns and instructions.

It is always fun to buy a home decor magazine to examine the photographs or read the articles that feature unusual needlework. *The World of Interiors,* an English publication, has fabulous interior design features. *Martha Stewart Living* at times will feature monogrammed linens and needlework projects that are in very good taste. Also check out *Country Living* and *Victoria* magazines, which show samples of old needlework pieces that are very inspiring as well.

For the Aspiring Amateur: Bookstores and Libraries

Books catering to needleworkers abound at your local bookstore and at book-selling giants like Barnes & Noble and Borders. Stores typically inventory a wide variety of books on all types of needlework, including embroidery and needlepoint. After you've explored the techniques in this book, it makes sense to buy a book that zeroes in on your taste, budget, and time. There are also some beautiful and grand picture books that are good coffee-table material.

If you do not live near a bookstore with a large inventory, small local bookstores can order any book you may desire. If you are on the Internet, check out Amazon.com and BN.com, which tend to keep their shipping costs relatively low. For a really good deal, peruse your magazines for book clubs that cater to needleworkers or crafts. Book clubs offer books at discounted retail prices but also often require that you order more than one title.

Public libraries are the best sources for free books, magazines, and videos (some are free or as little as $1.00 to rent) on every subject about needlework. The only drawback is that there is a time limit on how long you can hold on to library materials—usually one week for new books and magazines and a month for older books. Videos are usually lent for a three-day period. If you would like to add a publication or video to your own library, copy the author's name, the title, and publishing or manufacturing firm. If it's a book, also note the ISBN (International Standard Book Number), found on the copyright page. You can order a copy through a bookstore. For a fee, magazine publishers are happy to send you back issues as well.

You can also check out secondhand bookstores where wonderful bargains are to be had.

Here are a few books I recommend:

Brittain, Judy. *The Step by Step Needlecraft Encyclopedia*. Dorling Kindersley, 1997.

Fassett, Kaffe. *Welcome Home*. Martingale & Company, 1999.

Good Housekeeping Illustrated Book of Needlecrafts. Carroll & Brown Limited/Hearst Corporation, 1994.

Time-Life Books. *American Country Needle Arts*. Rebus, Inc., 1990.

Thorne-Thomsen, Kathleen, and Hildy Paige Burns. *American Cross Stitch*. Van Nostrand Reinhold Co., 1974.

Window-Shopping for Ideas

Browsing through model rooms in large department stores can be a real treat. Big stores like Bloomingdale's, Macy's, and Neiman-Marcus offer well-appointed home furnishings that are detailed with accessories like wall hangings, pillows, and linens, some of which may be embroidered or needlepointed. Critique the way these items are stitched and displayed. Add these styles to your memory bank, or sketch what you like and add to your files.

Some stores devote themselves to a particular look and clientele. Ralph Lauren Home Store (especially the one in New York City) boasts floors of luxurious furnishings, which usually include some needleworked items—all with a well-bred air and high-ticket prices! If you see even one pillow that you like, it will start your creativity flowing; even if the goods are not in your budget, the trip through the store is worth it.

ABC Carpet and Home, also in New York City, is another visual delight. Fantastically classic and offbeat items mesh to make some of the most artistic displays around. Its inventory includes table linens, rugs, pillows, loads of textiles, and other items. You may pick up a design that just knocks you out!

Another great (and possibly more local) source worth noting is house tours. They are usually held during holidays or festive seasons. One local group, say, the garden club, may choose a home to dress up for holiday viewing. Not only do you see garlands and wreaths, but you may also get to see a rare piece of holiday needlework or the owners' collection of embroidered linens. Who knows unless you go! Call your local chamber of commerce to find out when and where the next house tour might be.

Professional showcases done by highly regarded interior designers are usually held at the end of April into the beginning of May. It is best to call and confirm showings. Here are a few:

➤ Kips Bay Boys and Girls Club Decorator Show House, New York, New York, 718-8933-8600

➤ The Atlanta Symphony Decorator Showhouse, Atlanta, Georgia, 404-733-4935

➤ The Kansas City Junior Women's Symphony Alliance Designers Showcase, Kansas City, Missouri, 913-345-0920

➤ The San Francisco Decorator Showcase, San Francisco, California, 415-749-6864

TV Shows and Home Videos

Don't change the channel when you see a show on cooking, travel, or home decor. Cooking shows may be shot on location in various regions and countries. Customs, foods, and entertaining may be discussed and photographed with native interiors that reveal local needlework. Travel shows often point out national museums, interior shots of homes of interest, and local dress. Both types of shows may provide studies of regional tastes and glimpses of tapestries, embroidered clothing, etc.

Lifestyle and learning channels are full of how-tos and tips on crafts and needlework. Check your local public broadcasting channel or TV guide to see when the home shows will be featured. They usually are shown nightly or on a weekly basis. If you'll miss a show on TV, videotape it for viewing later on when you have the time. Also, check out your local library or bookstore for the current informational shows that you can buy or rent. Lifetime TV with shows like *Handmade by Design* that feature all types of crafts, *Martha Stewart Living* TV show featuring "good things," as well as some home shows produced by PBS (Public Broadcasting System) and HGTV (Home and Garden Channel), all offering neat ideas on arts and crafts and home-related items.

Getting Plugged In and Online

With a computer, modem, and online software program (America Online, for example), you can get connected and start browsing for everything you always wanted to know about embroidery or needlepoint. You might even find yourself signed up for an online chat, trading ideas with other needlework enthusiasts.

Familiarize yourself with your computer and sign up for an Internet service. You can then search the Web for a cajillion sites that have information on embroidery or needlepoint and many other needlework subjects. Type in the subject that you're looking for and up on the screen will come sites with descriptions. Click on the ones of interest, and you will find quick and easy access to local and global needlework information.

Teach Yourself Through CD-ROMs

Now your computer can teach you a few things about needlework! For example, the thread company DMC puts out a CD-ROM that comes with a beginner kit of thread, fabric, pattern, and needle. Place the CD-ROM in your computer, and you'll be able to watch demonstrations of different steps to learn or improve your needlework techniques. You'll also see animated and interactive stitching tips and hints, plus step-by-step illustrations to practice stitching your kit. The CD-ROM will also have many charts that you can print out in color or black-and-white, as well as a color guide to DMC's threads.

Classes

If you feel you still need a bit more formal education, try taking a class through your local needlework shop, community center, or continuing education program. These are usually set up for a particular level of expertise and for a particular project. Classes are a fun way to learn the art of needlework, make new friends, and complete a project.

Whether your favorite resource is the neighborhood shop or chat rooms online, the best way to come across ideas and items for projects is to use the tools you had all along: your eyes and ears. An open mind helps, too!

Supplies: A Local and Global Source Guide

There are a plethora of places to get all of your supplies. Along with your local retail shop—which should be your first stop—there are other options. If you need items that are unavailable locally, almost everything is available on the Internet and through magazines. Check out these resources for an endless supply of needlework tools, kits, and materials.

Chain Stores and Specialty Shops

The large chain stores such as Wal-Mart, K-Mart, Michael's, and MJD have craft sections that include materials and kits for needlepoint and embroidery. Although the selection of threads, needles, and fabrics is limited at these stores, the kit choice is more extensive.

If you choose a kit, think back to Chapter 2, "Well-Designed Needle Art," in which you learned about design elements. Then critique the kit design for color, scale, balance, and texture. Match your personal style with the kit that you choose, and don't forget level of expertise. Some designs will be better than others. The prices are reasonable in chain stores, and it's not a bad idea to start with an affordable first-time project, with all of the materials included. Although the kits aren't unique, you can personalize them by stitching your initials, by choosing a different frame or finishing method, or by using your piece in a unique way. Hand-painted canvas, special luxurious styled yarns, or one-of-a-kind patterns are not available at a mass merchandiser. For unusual kits and better designs, try your local stitch shop.

A specialty shop can be a godsend when you are just learning about needlework. The owner is often a very enthusiastic needleworker and knowledgeable about your interests. The shop typically carries a selection of "better" goods and quality designer-oriented patterns and hard-to-find canvases. The staff can also help you from start to finish and in between with those emergency questions.

They will also help you match the right needle with the correct thread and fabric, and guide you in selecting a finishing method. The small shops are competing with large chain stores; so if you ask for help, be sure to help them out, too, by purchasing their goods. You may even get hooked on other types of needlework!

Here is a smattering of specialty shops around the country. Be sure to look through all the shops listed as most have Web sites and some specialize in certain areas of needlework. If you'd like to find more shops for a specific state, get online and type in www.about.com. Then go to "hobbies," then to "needlepoint" (or "cross stitch"). Check out the site for a complete listing of shops around the country. Most of the shops usually have items for embroidery as well. Just ask! Each site will have phone numbers and addresses.

Alabama

➤ Patches and Stitches, Huntsville

Arizona

➤ Golden Horse Needlepoint, Sedona

➤ Old Town Needlework, Old Town Scottsdale

➤ Quail Run Needlework, Inc., Scottsdale

California

➤ Helen's Hobbies, Torrance

➤ L.A. Stitchers, Los Angeles

➤ Needlepoint, Inc., San Francisco

➤ Nettie's Needlecraft, Beverly Hills

Colorado

➤ Diversions Needlepoint, Englewood

➤ The Needleworker, Denver

Connecticut

➤ Needlepoint Heaven, West Hartford

➤ Selma's Yarns and Needleworks, Southbury

Florida

➤ Needlepoint Originals, Fort Lauderdale

➤ A Stitch in Time, Jacksonville

Hawaii

➤ Needlepoint, Etc., Honolulu

Idaho

➤ Isabel's Needlepoint, Ketchum

Illinois

➤ Divine Needlepoint, Chicago

➤ Needlework Corner, Carbondale

➤ Perfect Touch Yarns, Joliet

Maine

➤ Stitchery Square, Camden

Maryland

➤ The Crafty Fox, Germantown

Massachusetts

➤ Vineyard Stitches, Martha's Vineyard

➤ Wellesley Needlepoint Collection, Wellesley

Minnesota

➤ The First and Last Stitch, St. Louis

Mississippi

➤ Stitch Niche Site Gulf Coast, Threadneedle Street, Ocean Springs

Nebraska

➤ Personal Threads, Omaha

New Jersey

➤ The Stitching Bee, Chatham

New Mexico

➤ Needlepoint Gallery, Santa Fe

New York

➤ Erica Wilson, Manhattan

North Carolina

➤ Corner Stitch and Frame, Outer Banks

➤ The French Knot, Raleigh

Ohio

➤ Stitches, Etc., Cleveland

Oklahoma

➤ Cyberstitchery, Norman

➤ Needlework Creations, Tulsa

Pennsylvania

➤ Olde Tollgate Stitchery, York

South Carolina

➤ Heirlooms, Myrtle Beach

➤ Nathalie May Needle Arts, Columbia

Tennessee

➤ Metamorphosis, Nashville

Texas

➤ Cottage Discount Needlework, Dallas

➤ The French Knot, Fort Worth

➤ Ginger's Needlearts and Framing, Austin

➤ Key Stitches, Dallas

➤ Merribee Needlearts and Crafts, Houston

Utah

➤ Needlepoint Joint, Ogden

Virginia

➤ the hook and i, Hampton Roads

➤ Hunt Country Yarns, Middleburg

Washington

➤ The Needlepointer, Seattle

➤ Parkside Wool Company, Bellevue

Canada

➤ Cross Stitch Cupboard, Ottawa

➤ Purple Needle, Calgary

➤ Silver Thimble, Ontario

➤ Stitches in Time, North Bay

➤ International Needlepoint and Cross Stitch, Nova Scotia

England

➤ Rose Cottage

Kit Designers and Manufacturers Online

Kits are often distributed under the manufacturer's name or a famous designer's name. Some designer kits are expensive but for good reason. They are meticulously designed by professionals and color-coordinated with fabulous patterns. The manufacturers' selections are good designs but without a designer name attached. These can all be found on the Internet with their own Web sites. Just plug in the company name or kit designer name, and the information will come up on your screen.

➤ Art Werk

➤ The Craft Project

➤ CraftNet Australia

➤ Crafts Heirloom Thumbnails

➤ Creative GeniusMaker

➤ Dakota Winds Needlepoint

➤ Sarah Davenport Victorian Tapestries

➤ Dimensions Needlepoint

➤ Kaffe Fassett Tapestry Kits

➤ Foxview Needlepoint

➤ Glorafilia

➤ Jolly Red Tapestry

➤ Landmark Tapestries

➤ Susan Lethbridge Designs

➤ Tortoise and Hare

➤ Majestic Merino

➤ Needlepoint Plus Plate Series

➤ Orna Silk Bangles

➤ Smiling Sheep Needlepoint

➤ The Stitchery

➤ Stitches Unlimited

➤ Sunset Needlepoint Kits

➤ Tapisseries de France

➤ Tapisseries de la Bucherie

➤ Tartanpoint Pillow Kits

➤ Vintage Meighan Needlepoint

➤ Erica Wilson Needlepoint Kits

➤ Your Favorite Waterway

Magazines

Magazines advertise suppliers and stores that carry all the needlework items you are looking for. Here are some favorites.

➤ *Classic Stitches*. Embroidery magazine based in Scotland

➤ *Craft & Needlework Age*. Geared to the professional designer and retail store owner

➤ *Cross Country Stitching*. Projects for the beginner to the experienced cross stitcher, with an emphasis on country-style and holiday designs

➤ *Cross Stitch Collection*. Geared toward the advanced needleworker

➤ *Cross Stitcher*. Britain's best-selling cross stitch magazine

➤ *Embroidery & Cross Stitch*. Australian based—lovely needlework

➤ *GLP International*. U.S. distributor for many European craft magazines

➤ *Just CrossStitch*. Published since the 1980s, lots of projects for the advanced beginner to experienced stitcher; also explores other types of needlework compatible with cross stitch

➤ *Needlecraft*. All types of needlework discussed—UK-based

➤ *Needlepoint Now* (USA). Bimonthly needle-art magazine

➤ *The Needleworker*. Beautiful needlework plus educational articles about finishing techniques, related types of needlework, and stitching techniques

➤ *Piecework*. A fascinating look at handwork across the ages and across the world; each issue is a treat

➤ *Plastic Canvas Home & Holiday*. Quick and easy home projects

➤ *Sampler & Antique Needlework Quarterly*. A special magazine, published quarterly, that focuses on antique needlework and tools, scholarly research articles, and sampler reproductions

➤ *Stitcher's World*. Features a fine variety of techniques, designs, and designers

➤ *Talking Threads*. South African bimonthly magazine about all types of needlework

➤ *Workbox* (UK). Articles about modern and traditional aspects of needlecrafts, textiles, and fabrics

➤ *Suite101.com/Cross Stitch*. Online magazine and resource list for cross stitchers

Finding It on the Web

It's as easy as dialing up, searching for, and going to the following sites to find all of the needlework items you can imagine. All this without ever leaving your home! Some even have pictures of the goods! Just type in the following names on your search engine and info for these sites will come on your screen. The whole point is to get the needleworker going to the Web and learning the process.

- **The Stitchery.** A popular needlework catalog online
- **A World of Needlepoint.** Low-priced, high-quality selection of canvases and fibers
- **Red Meadow Fiber Arts.** Artistic shop with good needlepoint selection
- **Rose Cottage.** Great site with extensive selection of British and American designers
- **The Secret Cupboard.** Online consignment store where you can buy and sell goods
- **Needlepoint.com.** Specializes in limited editions
- **Tentakulum.** German embroidery site
- **Tri Thy Needlecraft Centre.** Family-owned shop site from North Wales
- **Twynham Craft and Haberdashery.** English site with British scene kits and canvases
- **Willow Fabrics.** UK shop with a good selection of needlework kits, fibers, and supplies
- **Wool & Crafts.** Site with handsome needlepoint kits and yarns
- **Wye Needlecraft.** English shop with a good variety of designers and supplies

Some companies have online staff to answer your questions about merchandise. When you are ready to order, you typically fill out a form to place the order—all online! It's not even necessary to leave your home.

Going, Going, Gone: Online Auctions

If you are a collector of needlework, a good site to look up is eBay, at www.ebay.com. eBay is by far one of the busiest and largest online auction houses. You can peruse old needleworks for sale or even some needleworking tools up for grabs. Some rare samplers or embroidered clothing may be of interest, or tapestries that would round out your collection.

There are message boards, a glossary for auction terms, and bidding tips. Be careful, though, because a bid is legally binding—so be sure you really want what you're bidding on.

Software

Needlework software can help you with stitches and techniques, provide you with design and supply information, and allow you to print graph paper from your computer. Just about anything that applies to your new craft can be found in software.

Here are some places to find software that will help you design some fabulous needlework:

➤ **Computer Software for Crafters FAQ.** How to select software for designing needlework

➤ **Crafted Software Australia Produces StitchCraft.** Program for designing cross stitch, tapestry, and rug-hooking charts; free monthly cross stitch charts and chart viewer

➤ **Creative Craftware.** Produces DigiStitch for Windows 95

➤ **Graph Paper Printer for Windows.** Can print graph paper in many different grid sizes

➤ **HobbyWare.** Develops and markets Pattern Maker for cross stitch

➤ **The Needlecrafter's Computer Companion by Judy Heim.** Pages of information; includes two disks of software

➤ **Palm Databases.** Free floss and fiber databases for PalmPilot and Windows

➤ **XMaster Designer.** Counted cross stitch design program for Windows 95 or later (Germany)

Glossary

acid-free tissue   A tissue made without the chemicals that destroy fabric fibers.

appliqué   A small piece of fabric, cut into a shape, that is placed on a background fabric and stitched down with small, almost invisible, stitches, usually by hand.

Bargello   A classic needlepoint stitch that results in wavy or chevron-type patterns resembling flames.

baste   To sew with large temporary stitches.

beading needle   A fine needle with a sharp tip that is used for beadwork.

blackwork   A counted thread embroidery in which repetitive patterns are used to fill design areas. Traditionally black silk thread was worked on linen. Today many colors are used.

blocking   A process for straightening a misshapen needlework piece by realigning the threads of the ground fabric, in order to eliminate the distortion that occurred during stitching.

canvas   Mesh fabric with criss-crossing fibers that form a grid; used to stitch needlepoint.

colorfast   A descriptive term referring to dyed fabrics or threads that will not run when wet.

couching   An embroidery technique by which a lighter-weight thread and small stitches are used to attach a heavier thread that has been laid flat on the surface of a ground fabric. Traditionally used to apply fragile metallic threads to a design.

crewel needle   Sharp pointed, medium-length needles with large eyes for easy threading.

crewelwork   A traditional form of embroidery, typically employing wool thread and linen twill fabric, flowing designs, and stylized naturalistic motifs executed with various stitches.

cross stitch   A popular embroidery stitch where all of the stitches are formed by two "crossing arms."

cutwork   A form of openwork embroidery where outlined designs are stitched with a buttonhole stitch and the middle is cutaway.

dressmaker's carbon paper   A type of coated paper used to transfer designs to fabric.

embroidery   A form of needlework that embellishes clothing or fabric with stitching.

evenweave   A woven fabric that has the same number of vertical threads as horizontal threads.

flat stitches   Embroidery stitches that lie flat on the surface of a fabric.

floss   An embroidery thread composed of six loosely twisted strands that are easily separated into single threads.

ground fabric   The background fabric of which needlework is done.

hoop   A round, portable, and lightweight frame used in needlework to keep the ground fabric taut during stitching.

intersection   A needlepoint term that refers to the intersecting points in the canvas grid.

joining   A process in which two sections of needlepoint canvas are sewn together.

matte   A finish that is not shiny.

monogram   In embroidery, a decorative rendering of a person's initials that is stitched on fabric.

mounting   The process of preparing to frame your work by securing it to a supporting board before attaching the actual frame.

needlepoint   A form of embroidery where canvas mesh fabric is stitched with yarn.

openwork   A type of embroidery where the stitches pull the fabric threads together creating open, lace like patterns.

pearle cotton   A strong twisted nondivisible thread with a high sheen.

Persian yarn   Loosely twisted three-strand wool or acrylic yarn that is easily divisible.

pile   A furry-looking effect achieved by using various looped stitches on a ground fabric. The loops are sometimes sheared to resemble the pile of a rug.

sampler   Originally, a piece of linen on which the embroiderer tried out and recorded various motifs and stitches for later use as a reference. In the eighteenth and nineteenth centuries, samplers became popular methods for teaching children their alphabet and numbers. Modern samplers typically still incorporate the alphabet while often commemorating a special occasion such as a birth, wedding, anniversary, or friendship.

satin stitch   A flat, straight, basic embroidery stitch. Satin stitches are placed close together, side by side, and are characterized by an equal amount of thread covering the front and the back of the fabric.

smocking   An embroidery technique that reduces fullness in a fabric with very attractive gathered stitches.

stumpwork   A seventeenth-century technique that makes embroidery three-dimensional by combining padded appliqué and embroidery stitches. Sometimes a fine wire is used to provide the underlying support and to give shape.

tapestry   A heavy, decoratively woven fabric with a pictorial design, traditionally used as a wall hanging.

tapestry needle   Blunt-tipped needles used for thread counting embroidery and needlepoint.

tent   A basic needlepoint stitch that is worked on the diagonal and in the same direction over one intersection of canvas.

tramé   A technique used on needlepoint canvas in which horizontal stitches are run across each part of the design to add thickness and strength to the canvas. The tramming is done before the canvas is retailed, and the stitcher then completes it by working needlepoint stitches over the tramming.

whitework   The name given to any white embroidery used on a white ground fabric.

Index